Betty Shine was born in Kennington in 1929. Her grandmother was a spiritualist. Before she became a practising healer, she was a professional singer, and she has at times taught vitamin and mineral therapy, hand analysis and yoga. She lives and practises in the south of England. Since publication of her first book, *Mind to Mind*, she has made numerous television appearances. *Mind Waves*, her new book, is now available in hardcover from Bantam Press.

Also by Betty Shine

MIND TO MIND

and published by Corgi Books

MIND MAGIC

The Key to the Universe

Betty Shine

CORGI BOOKS

MIND MAGIC
A CORGI BOOK 0 552 13671 9

Originally published in Great Britain by Bantam Press,
a division of Transworld Publishers Ltd.

PRINTING HISTORY
Bantam Press edition published 1991
Corgi edition published 1992
Corgi edition reprinted 1992
Corgi edition reprinted 1993

This book is set in 11/13pt Sabon by
Falcon Typographic Art Ltd., Edinburgh & London

Corgi Books are published by Transworld Publishers Ltd.,
61–63 Uxbridge Road, Ealing, London W5 5SA, in Australia
by Transworld Publishers (Australia) Pty. Ltd., 15–25 Helles
Avenue, Moorebank, NSW 2170, and in New Zealand
by Transworld Publishers (N.Z.) Ltd., 3 William Pickering
Drive, Albany, Auckland.

Printed and bound in Great Britain by
Cox & Wyman Ltd., Reading, Berkshire

To Alan, for his love, support and for always being there

Acknowledgements

To my editor, Rivers Scott, for his skill, charm and humour. And to Janet Shine and Wanda Woolgar without whom my office would be chaos.

Contents

Introduction

My first book *Mind to Mind* has reached out to the far corners of the world and formed a community of kindred spirits. This has become obvious from the thousands of letters I have received from people from all walks of life, not just thanking me for writing the book but saying that it has changed their lives.

Mind Magic will take you further along the path to independence and awareness.

The Imagination is the Key to the Universe. With your own key you will be able to unlock the door to experiences you will never forget.

The exercises in this book are extremely powerful – do not be deceived by their apparent simplicity. The methods I teach have been tried and tested over many years and are absolutely safe. Try them. Your life will never be the same again.

Part One

HEALING

One

MIND ENERGY

What comfort, what strength, what economy there is in order – material order, intellectual order, moral order. To know where one is going and what one wishes – this is order; to keep one's word and one's engagements – again order; to have everything ready under one's hand, to be able to dispose of all one's forces, and to have all one's means of whatever kind under command – still order; to discipline one's habits, one's efforts, one's wishes; to organize one's life, to distribute one's time – all this belongs to and is included in the word order. Order means light and peace, inward liberty and free command over oneself. Order is power.

Henri-Frédérique Amiel (1821–81)

This book is called MIND MAGIC and that is exactly what it is going to be about – MIND and MAGIC, or rather, what at first sight looks like magic. So here, to start off, are two stories which seem to be about magic. I will show you why they are actually about mind.

The first concerns an appearance of mine on Southern Sound, the radio station at Portslade, Brighton, in Sussex, quite near my home. My engagement was on that popular programme *The Eleventh Hour* presented by Peter Quinn, whose interest in the paranormal led him to devise this show on which people like myself are invited to explain their theories. Peter and I have since become great friends. I doubt, however, whether he bargained for what would happen on that occasion, or would ever again want to repeat the experience!

The broadcast took place at eleven o'clock at night. I sat down, adjusted the microphone, and the interview began. I was talking about mind control and repeated many times how powerful the mind can be. Then suddenly, the console with all the controls started flashing, the television monitor blacked out, and the studio became very hot. Peter Quinn looked dazed. He became red in the face and started twisting about in the heat. 'My God!' he said, looking up at the creaking ceiling. 'What's happening?'

We got through the interview somehow and as I emerged from the studio, I found a scene of even greater confusion. The whole building was blacked out, fire and burglar alarms were ringing, electric doors had locked themselves, never again, it seemed, to be unlocked! A police car, summoned by the burglar alarms, had driven up. Peter Quinn, still at his post, and trying to run two stations in these conditions, was going berserk. 'Everything has blown up,' he kept saying to the listeners. 'I'm getting hotter by the minute.' Two hours later he was still waiting for the electricians to turn up and still repeating to his listeners, 'Betty Shine has gone, leaving me in total darkness.'

It transpired that the station's electricity supply had blown, two out of its three emergency generators had gone out of action, and the air-conditioning had packed it in. But the studio in which I had given my talk was left with power, the only one to be so. Coincidence? I don't think so. I was protected because, in this broadcast, I was spreading the word.

The second experience, even stranger than the one at the studio, occurred more recently and concerned my friend the actor Michael Crawford, star of *Phantom of the Opera*. I had been thinking a lot about him – thinking about him very intensely, in fact, as he was about to embark on another important phase in his career. Suddenly his voice singing *The Music of the Night*, his main song in the show, came bursting out from the record player.

I looked at it in amazement. I had certainly not switched it on or set the record playing. In fact, I had not used it for weeks. Then I looked down at the wall. The record was on the turntable but the machine was not even plugged in. There was no electricity. My own resources had supplied the power!

How does one generate power like this? The answer is, by MIND ENERGY.

In my first book, *Mind to Mind*, I explained how I discovered a bright, white energy around the head which looked like a vibrating halo and which I had studied for eleven years. I explained how negative thought funnelled this energy inwards instead of outwards, while positive thought directed it outwards instead of inwards. In so doing it expanded it in ever more powerful ways, linking it up with the universal mind, that great reservoir of thought and knowledge outside ourselves.

Healing is dependent on the application of mind energy; so are thought transference, clairvoyance, mediumship and much else. If I say that mind energy is the great force in our lives I am not exaggerating. Its power is even greater than that of the atom – after all, it harnessed it – and like the atom it must be used only for good, because whatever you give out will return to you tenfold or more. That is the Universal Law. There is no getting away from it. Whatever you give out will, no matter how long it takes, return.

I have spent many years studying this energy around the heads of hundreds of clients and this study was my main reason for writing my bestselling book. I wanted to share my discoveries with the whole world. Now my desire is to go one stage further. I hope this present book will give you a still better understanding of mind energy and why it is vital to be positive at all times, why you cannot allow negativity into your life. I will not only explain in it how mediums receive messages and give evidence of survival, how absent healing is given, how the Universal Mind links up with the intuition, but also how you can become psychic, have your own survival messages and clairvoyance, heal yourself and others and also give absent healing. By the time you have finished reading it you should already have opened the door to a new, positive, optimistic life-style.

But first I want you to remember that mind energy

is affected by every single thought you have. So let us get back to mind energy.

When someone is depressed it looks as though the whole centre of the halo I described has been sucked in. Knowing how powerful this energy is, one can only guess at the pressure that must be depressing the brain and surrounding muscles and tissue. It is quite dangerous, to say the least, and the more you can work at lifting the pressure and return the halo to its natural shape, the healthier you will be. If you are a natural depressive, please don't worry – there is still a way out. This book has been written with you in mind.

Try to think outwards at all times. Thinking of oneself all the time is a bad habit that has to go – believe me, you cannot afford it and, let's face it, it really is quite simple. Remember, inward thinking draws the mind energy down. Outward thinking expands it, releasing pressures.

For example, we have all noticed how our memory is affected when times are difficult and negativity creeps in. This is because the brain cells are under pressure and cannot function correctly. When this pressure is very bad, the messages which the brain gives to the body to enable it to function can sometimes be incorrect, and this can cause a number of physical problems which are called psychosomatic. In this case healing can work miracles by simply dislodging the congestion caused by the mind energy. Now you can see how important it is to be positive, to keep the mind energy expanding outwards and to keep the pressure off the brain and body.

I can hear you saying, it's OK for you; you haven't got my life. Believe me, my life has been full of problems and there are very few people indeed who escape. Life itself is problematical. If it were easy we wouldn't strive; we wouldn't learn to progress in any way. We all need the stimulation of challenge as well as our quiet moments. Everything has to be balanced.

That is why I am not asking you *never* to be negative; only to limit the negativity to a short period. If you can't solve your problem at once, then time yourself and switch off after five minutes. In that five minutes you can think logically about the situation but don't dwell on the fact that you cannot alter it. Switch off after five minutes. If your thoughts return quickly, tell them to push off. And be quite adamant about it. After all, no matter what has befallen you, you still have your life to live and you must, for your own salvation, get on with it.

Later in the day, if you wish, have another five minutes negativity, but only five minutes. Don't forget to switch off. If at some later date you find the answer to your problem it will be because you did not allow the mind energy to funnel in and take away the sharpness of your logical thought. Remember, the mind energy is the power and the brain the computer. Without the power, the computer is useless. If you find this difficult try the blackboard exercise that will come later in the book.

Now you have a little knowledge about mind energy, let me tell you more. This same energy actually leaves the body when you die. I have seen it leave. It can take on many shapes but it cannot be destroyed because it is energy. It joins an energy dimension. That is why mediums with their expansive mind energy can link up with minds in other dimensions and have a mind-to-mind contact with those who have died.

A medium cannot contact a particular mind and receive messages. The contact must first be made from the energy dimension. Once this contact has been made, then we can pass on messages. The contact however can be broken from both sides. If the medium returns to menial tasks, then the expansion of mind energy is reduced and the contact ceases. That is why a good medium is always entirely positive when giving evidence, keeping the mind energy going for ever outwards and linking it up with the universal mind. The messages received and given will then be messages of quality. The quantity is of no importance at all.

What is the Universal Mind? It is a collection of past minds, of minds strengthened with knowledge, talent and spiritual values, and it is a source that can be tapped by anyone wishing to seek knowledge. Once you have the secret of tapping the universal mind, life becomes easier. But beware. You will also learn spiritual values and gradually lose your desire for unnecessary material objects. However, you will also be happier and healthier. That has to be a great bonus. I will tell you how, if you sit quietly, close your eyes, and do the following exercise, you can make life easier for yourself.

Feel comfortable and relaxed. Let yourself go. Allow your mind to drift away, to visit some far-off land, to sit on a mountain top or by the sea, listening to the crash of the waves as they hit the shoreline and rocks. Maybe walking through a sunlit valley glowing with the beautiful reds and oranges of wild poppies would be more to your liking. Whatever your choice, allow your mind to linger there for a while. Remember: the mind is energy and it can travel anywhere in the world. The thought is the deed and with another single thought you can bring it back. Practise projecting and retracting your mind energy and you will notice how light you feel when your thoughts are miles away.

When you feel thoroughly rested I would like you to try another small exercise that will take you into the centre of the universe. You will be visiting the centre of all wisdom. Imagine a pin-point of light in a darkened sky, think yourself towards it, and as you travel with the speed of lightning you will see it getting bigger and bigger until you find yourself at the opening of a tunnel. Go through the tunnel and you will emerge into the Great Hall of Knowledge where wise men (The Ancients) will be seated around a half-circle table. Walk toward the table and you will see a chair. Sit down, close your eyes, and listen to the silence, the audible silence, for the wise men will be communicating with you telepathically.

22

Open your eyes. Little by little the knowledge and teachings you have been given will be impressed upon the physical brain and you will surprise yourself by solving your own problems. Life will become a lot easier and you will find a peace never before experienced.

If you are unable to see through the imagination, because of a lack of vitality in your mind energy (this is a common problem), please don't worry. Just know that it is happening. It will still have the same effect.

The sudden dawning of the knowledge received in this way can be called intuition. Whether you know it or not, intuition is the result of linking up with the Universal Mind, whether by intention or accident.

Talents become stronger, more powerful, when someone has a positive, expansive mind energy. Artists are for ever looking outwards, away from themselves, as are sculptors, singers, musicians, surgeons, anyone who is a giver rather than a taker. The more outward-thinking you are, the more expansive the mind energy and the more you will link up with the knowledge of the Universal Mind.

There is no doubt that to survive in the world as it is today we need to call upon energies to sustain us and guide us. It is becoming increasingly difficult to exist without this aid. The expansion of mind energy is therefore a must for those who want to remain healthy and successful. Negativity can become an incurable disease. It is certainly a habit that is all too easily acquired. Learning positivity demands time and effort at first, but take my word for it, the moment will come when it is just a part of your everyday routine.

Then, no longer will you have tension headaches, aches and pains all over your body, overactive adrenalin glands, bad circulation and the many other complaints with which most of us nowadays live as a matter of course. People have forgotten what it is like to be 100 per cent healthy – especially young people. When you feel really healthy, achieving becomes your goal. Believing in yourself seems natural and you have no hang-ups or tensions. Life is great and you feel great. But how many of my readers, I wonder, starting out on this book, are feeling like that? Very few, I suspect.

Since *Mind to Mind* was published I have received letters about the book from over 40,000 readers. Almost without exception, they have said that it has changed their lives – proof in itself that what I am teaching works!

In that book I added a few simple exercises with the intention of encouraging readers to start experimenting with my methods themselves. The exercises I shall be giving you now are intended to take you into the next class, to encourage you to risk a further leap into the unknown and to help you find out for yourself who you are. You may be surprised to find within yourself gifts you never knew you possessed, a spirituality of which you never suspected even the seeds, emotions you never dreamed of. The pages that follow will explore unknown territory, offering the most exciting adventure imaginable – and all without leaving the comfort of your own home! The wisdom of the ancients is always a challenge:

> Without leaving his door
> He knows everything under heaven.
> Without looking out of his window
> He knows all the ways of heaven.
> The further one travels
> The less one knows.
> Therefore the sage arrives without going,
> Sees all without looking,
> Does nothing, achieves everything.

Tao Te Ching

Tao Te Ching is, of course, speaking about the mind!

So much more was known about mind power in those days. The building of the pyramids! The discovery of meridian lines in acupuncture! Stonehenge, constructed without modern technology. The great uprights – the sarsens – of that formidable array of stones weigh 50 tons each. Thirty of them were originally arranged in a 1,000-foot circle, inside which there were sixty 'bluestones' each weighing 5 tons. How were these sarsens shaped? Sarsen is so hard that modern steels have no effect on it. We think that as far as technology is concerned we are streets ahead of the ancients. Believe me, in many ways we are light years behind them!

How is it that churches all over the country are built where ley lines meet? (Ley lines are a network of earth forces that criss-cross the land and, where

SARSENS X

they join, these churches, barrows and prehistoric sites are found. Stonehenge, in particular, is at the centre of geodetic lines). Hundreds of years ago people used their natural psychic power – that is, their mind power – to chart the ley lines. These people were normal. It is people without psychic power who are abnormal. They have lost their way because they have no guide lines, no energy lines to grasp. They have no intuition and once intuition has been lost human beings become like sheep, following one another and hoping to God that someone, somewhere, has the right ideas.

Where are the great explorers, those wonderful people with a superabundance of courage who ventured into the unknown with a donkey and a pack? Using their intuition they walked the ley lines without knowing they were doing so. It came so naturally to them. They had no wish to change the people they found, or their environment. They only wanted to see and become a part of something new and strange to them, even if they thought it uncivilized – something exciting.

The one thing they failed to realize was that the people they met were way ahead of them in respect of natural law, Universal Law, and an instinctive survival system. These people knew instinctively when other tribes were about to visit them, as much as a week ahead! How could this be? The only answer is mind power, the power of thought transference, and the ability of mind energy to travel over long distances.

I would like to tell you a little about Sri Sathya Sai Baba, a remarkable man and a saint, who performs miracles every day of the year – miracles which have been witnessed by men of integrity and power from all over the world. Red-hot objects rise from the sand, flowers are turned into jewels, rocks into sweets, material objects are manifested from thin air, as also is *vibhuti*, a sacred ash used for healing. I could fill this book with the miracles of Sai Baba but instead will confine myself to one story.

A patient of mine who was a follower of this sage visited one of his ashrams in England. Whilst she was there a man put his hand on her shoulder and said, 'You have a friend who is a healer?' She replied, 'Yes.' The man then said, 'The Master wishes her to have these.' Whereupon he handed her a bag containing dozens and dozens of packets of the precious *vibhuti*, plus a photograph of Sai Baba, a locket with a photograph of him, and another of the person he had been in a previous life. To say that my patient was flabbergasted would be to understate her reaction. But she duly handed the packets to me, wondering why I should have them and not herself, the disciple.

Since then this incredible man has appeared to me twice, with ten years, at least, intervening between the two visits. His last visit was quite recent and occurred when I had raging toothache for three days. It was a holiday period and I couldn't get to a dentist. It was only the help of my Mind Medicine Room that kept me sane. While I was lying on the bed wondering how I could give a lecture in two days, Sai Baba appeared and gave me an assurance that I would be out of pain the next day. I just couldn't believe this – which shows how much further along the road to enlightenment I had (and still have) to go!

I got up next morning still in agony and thought, 'So much for that prophecy.' Janet, my daughter, who is not a professional healer, came to visit me and I said, 'Look I know you aren't a healer but with all of your psychic power why don't you have a go, give me some healing?' This she did and I had a miraculous cure.

This is how mind power works. Messages are relayed in all sorts of ways and clearly I was prompted to ask Janet for help so that the miracle healing could be carried out through her. We are all used, in one way or another, make no mistake about that. If we listen to our intuition and are guided by it, problems are overcome in a seemingly miraculous way. There is always someone wishing to link up with your mind and help you, but unless you meet that person halfway you will not receive the message the helper is trying to give you. By carrying out the exercises in this book you will be able to meet your helper halfway. And it will change your life!

Sai Baba lives in Puttaparti in India and has always said that he will never visit the West because we are not ready for him. He is right, but what a tragedy! Perhaps one day he will change his mind. Let us hope so anyway. I have never been a follower of

Sai Baba and never will be. I have always taken an independent path. But my respect for him could not be greater and when people tell me how incredible my gifts are, I only have to think of him to know that I still have a long way to go, possibly a few more lifetimes. Having said that, I find it exciting to start people along the road of progression and to pass on what knowledge I have. We all have to start somewhere, and most people haven't even opened the first gate!

Sai Baba says that his gifts are his visiting cards that send him instant flashes when someone is ill. That was certainly true in my case. Yet in between his two visits I have had little time to think about him. And in fact, there is no need. We don't go around all day, every day, thinking about God and neither should we. It is enough to know He is there, and that is the same with Sai Baba. I also know there is no need for me to visit India to see him because my mind can travel effortlessly anywhere in the world.

I hope by now that you are beginning to feel excited about your own future mind journeys and what your own, unique experiences will be. I am certainly excited for you because I know that, without my own experiences of this sort, my life would have been extremely dull.

That is why I think it is such a pity that most scientists only see the world of matter. Their minds are only half open; indeed, the minds of some of them are quite closed. If they were to expand their minds perhaps they would find a way of saving our planet. They cannot do this unless they see the world as a whole. Some scientists, I know, have broken through this barrier, only to be shunned by their peers as a result. If we can reinforce the strength of the few by improving the efforts of the many then we too will have played a major part in reversing the breakdown of the ecology.

Do not be put off by literature that assures you that mind energy does not exist. I know that it does because I can see it and have studied it. Simply try the exercises printed in this book and prove its existence for yourself. Do not live your life through others. Experience it for yourself.

In my first book I explained how the energy system in its varying manifestations is today becoming increasingly accepted. Many of the alternative or complementary methods of healing – acupuncture, for instance – have been based on those principles for centuries, and those of us who constantly use and work with energy experience 'miracles' every day – another example of the magic that is in fact mind. But besides the positivity that expands it and drives it on, mind energy itself requires one activating and controlling force. That force is IMAGINATION.

To start with, most people probably think of imagination as something spontaneous, vague and undirected. Imagination of the kind I am talking about is exactly the opposite. Imagination – that is, the deliberate making of images – is the producer and expander of mind energy. Far from allowing it to come and go at its own whim, you deliberately seek to set it going and control it, to nurture and enlarge it in every way you can.

By building up pictures you are strengthening mind energy until its powers are almost limitless. The exercises in this book are designed for just that purpose – to enable you to manipulate the mind energy through the imagination. Through the exercises, I shall be teaching you how to expand mind energy, how to keep the pressure off the brain and body, and how this discipline will open up your whole life.

This is your own mind effort. There is also a magical point. When you build up pictures in this way by use of the controlled imagination you are at the same time beaming them out into space. In due course somebody out there will beam back to you pictures of their own, clairvoyant visions which will help you along your path. Jung understood this. He was a man who never wasted a vision. He always accepted it as part of his own clairvoyance and acted upon it.

This book will teach you many other disciplines, the result of which will be to bring about a valuable increase in mind energy. How to rest properly, how to supplement your food, how to make friends with our wonderful natural environment and not to join those who seem to be hell-bent on wrecking it – all these are important lessons. Through them you will learn how to tap knowledge from the universal mind and enhance your life in all its aspects. After all, not all of us wish to expend our energies blowing fuses in broadcasting studios or getting sounds out of record players without the bother of plugging them in. Those are just the trimmings!

The aim of this book is to 'plug you in' in a different way. Imagination is the controlling force behind mind energy. It is also the key to your health, happiness and success. Through it you can grow roots, driving them deep into the soil just as though you were a great oak, so that never again will you be rocked about when things are bad. You will become independent. You will have freedom of thought, word and deed. Moreover, as time goes on, you will become a better person, kinder, more spiritual, in harmony with nature and with your family and friends.

You don't have to believe me. Just try my methods and see! This is a do-it-yourself, be-your-own-alchemist book, a complete self-help manual for the body and for the mind, and I guarantee that by the end of it you will be amazed by the person you seem to have become. *An undisciplined mind will always be the servant of a disciplined mind.* That is another Universal Law. Make sure, then, that *your* mind is disciplined! Put to good use, the imagination can transform our lives. With it we can go out tomorrow and start changing the world. We can also fight a war against ill-health in ourselves and others because among the things we can change are our own and their cellular systems.

In the next chapter I will start telling you how the healing process works.

Two

THE MECHANICS OF THE ENERGY COUNTERPART

(On earth there is nothing great but man; in man there
is nothing great but mind.)

Sir William Hamilton (1788–1856),
Lectures on Metaphysics

I lie on the couch, nice and warm. Betty explains about
her healing and lays those lovely warm hands on my body.
Without further ado she mentions that she is being told I
have a malformed kidney. I look around stupidly for the
person who is telling her this but of course she is speaking
spiritually. She places her hands on my right kidney and
confirms the diagnosis. Then she tells me that I also have
skin cancer. She is correct, yet no signs of this condition
are visible. She also suggests that I have problems with
my eyes, an ulcer and enzyme deficiency – all correct!
Betty Shine had been told that I had multiple sclerosis
but nothing at all about my state of health apart from
that. How could she diagnose all these symptoms with
such accuracy?

The patient who wrote these words, Peter Williams,
a successful but sceptical businessman, had been
invited to take part in a television programme
about the powers of mediums and healers, and
he also agreed to be filmed again later on to see
if his health had improved. When I first saw him,
his physical state was appalling. He could not walk

except with a stick or supported by his wife Shirley. He knocked into furniture, spilled drinks all over the tray, and suffered from a weak bladder. In fact, he was a wreck. He had also been told that he had only a short time to live and was inclined to believe this.

After six visits to me he was shopping in Croydon for the first time in ten years. This first outing lasted two hours and his wife spent a fortune! His eyes, skin, kidney and bladder were better and his friends and colleagues, not to mention the producer of the television programme, were all astonished at his progress.

Yet his question remains: How had I diagnosed him? Before answering, I must pause to give a brief description of the process by which the clairvoyant healer does his or her work.

All life is energy, and fitting neatly into the physical system is the ENERGY COUNTERPART, which mirrors it on the non-physical plane. The aura – a word much used but little understood – is an extension of the energy counterpart. It protrudes about an inch and a half all round the physical body when the latter is healthy and, along with the energy counterpart, virtually disappears and becomes invisible when it is not. A unique gift that has been bestowed upon me is the ability to 'see' this energy. The most important components of the energy counterpart are the vortices, or chakras, to give them their Hindu name, and meridian lines.

The vortices appear opposite the ductless glands in the endocrine system. Their function is to draw in life force and stimulate the glands' hormonal output. When the body is healthy these vortices spin at great speed. When it is sick they begin to slow down, drawing in life force at a diminishing rate and setting up a vicious circle. For if, as already explained, our mind energy begins to funnel inwards instead of expanding outwards, a congestion of energy gradually forms in the body, the major organs are prevented from pulsating, cells and tissues suffer and tremendous negative pressure builds up, affecting in its turn the energy counterpart and aura which, as explained, retracts into the body and becomes invisible. The healer's first task in this situation is to get the vortices spinning again. This can be done by energizing the system through healing until they are once more turning with the sparkle and speed of Catherine wheels.

As well as the vortices, the energy counterpart displays a whole network of what are known as meridian lines. These are energy lines that channel life force through the physical body. I have no idea how many meridian lines there are, but there are quite a few, some of which I have seen. To clear them I draw the energy back through the feet rather as a pipe smoker uses his pipe cleaner. This also reactivates the vortices. Acupuncture, in the hands of a skilled practitioner, has the same effect. As the needles are inserted into the physical body, they release negative congestion from the energy counterpart.

Many books offer line drawings claiming to illustrate the position of the vortices. This book will not offer you charts or sketches of anything, for the reason that I want you to exercise your imagination and, by so doing, expand your mind energy. But I recognize that many people find such visualization difficult, particularly at the start. If you are one of them, try the following exercise.

Sit down, close your eyes, and imagine that you are transparent. You can see, or imagine, an outline of your physical body. Moving down it slowly from the top front of your head, observe the first vortex spinning like a Catherine wheel. Now move to just about the middle of the forehead. Here is another vortex, slightly elongated in shape this time, but also spinning away at its centre. Now to the throat. Have another look at these three vortices. If by now your imagination is flagging, just accept that they are all there, spinning away.

Now we come to the heart vortex, at the centre of the breastbone, then to the vortex situated just over the pancreas, then to another just below it, at the level of the navel.

Now turn your energy being around, so that it has its back to you. Here is the seventh and last main vortex, situated at the base of the spine. This is the *kundalini*, the 'earth vortex', drawing its strength from the earth's energies.

So here you have, in your mind's eye, a picture of your energy counterpart, your transparent frame with its seven spinning vortices.

Now turn your energy being around to face you again and look down at its feet. Lift your gaze slowly up the body's left side, right up to the shoulder, and you will see channels of energy, maybe two or three. These are your meridian lines. Starting with the right foot and rising to the right shoulder, you will see the same thing. Perhaps it will be easier for you to visualize these channels as tubes. Now let your energy being raise its arms. From beneath the armpits there are tubes going down both arms. There are also many channels tracing a course across the chest and back and up through the neck into the head.

Vortices spinning and drawing in life force, channels or meridians distributing this life force, the whole energy being vibrating and pulsating – that is what your energy counterpart should look like and therefore how you should visualize it while controlling it.

Now, imagine you are entering this wonderful, vibrating energy being. Simply walk into it and, if it adds to your sense of security, zip yourself up at the back. Suddenly this energy will take on the shapes of all your major organs, curling around them, mimicking them, and regenerating every cell in your body. Now you are feeling on top of the world because you are fit and healthy and bubbling over with the energy.

Do not underestimate the energy counterpart or dismiss it as mere fantasy. It is not. It is as real as our physical bodies which, without it, could not exist. When our vortices are spinning we are healthy and full of life, when they are slow disease sets in and when they stop we die.

Most people jog along with slow vortices all their lives. They show little interest in how their physical bodies work, let alone their energy counterparts. But such neglect exacts a penalty and this falls due when they are ill. Then they feel out of control. Along comes the doctor with his usual well-meaning prescriptions. But the drugs he prescribes will only slow the vortices down even more, while their chemical reaction will alter the messages from the brain, thereby leading to more problems.

How much safer to play down the physical side and concentrate from the first on manipulating the energy counterpart, starting even when you are well – it is so much easier to control and the physical body will benefit as a matter of course.

All you have to remember is that there are seven vortices, perhaps more. Don't worry about where they are. Just be convinced that they exist and are spinning like Catherine wheels while drawing in life force. The same with the meridian lines. Don't worry about them. Just assure yourself that they are there and are conducting the life force around the body.

So I come back to the question with which I began: How did I diagnose Peter Williams's various illnesses? The answer is: by examining his energy counterpart. Once you have a clear picture of the mind energy and energy counterpart and how they should work it is fairly easy to diagnose abnormalities. Later I will teach you how to carry out your own diagnosis by touch.

After his healing sessions Peter sent me his own

account of them. I think you will find it fascinating. He wrote:

Through the glass door I can see Betty walking towards us, a very attractive, mature lady with a warm smile. She radiates so much personality that you immediately feel comfortable in her presence. If I had but a few moments to live I would choose this lady to be at my side. No wonder people feel better after seeing her.

Betty prescribed herbal remedies, both to improve my digestion and to relieve my problems of stomach acidity, namely Papaya Enzyme and Acidophilus plus Pectin, both available at the local health shop. After my first three sessions I was a little disappointed. There were no dramatic improvements.

Where was the miracle cure? Afterwards I realized I was being totally unfair. I was looking for a miracle and in so doing overlooked the beneficial changes that later became apparent.

Even more total was my misjudgement of Betty herself. Here is a lady who is dedicated to her cause, very intelligent, knowledgeable, and experienced in character assessment, with a dynamic personality. She frequently roars with laughter, which is infectious; and soon I was under her spell.

During my fourth healing session I was lying on the couch feeling far more relaxed, as Betty now had my full respect, when I felt a noticeable click in my spine. I did not mention this at the time. But talking about it later to Shirley my wife, she confirmed that other patients of Betty's had experienced this sensation while undergoing treatment.

During the following week I witnessed vast improvements in my health generally. My kidney gave me much less aggravation, my eyes cleared (they were often quite bloodshot), my skin looked more alive (I had often appeared quite pale), colour came back to my cheeks and I was becoming more mobile. I looked forward to my sessions with Betty more and more each time, and after a few more visits my walking improved dramatically.

Amazing things happened during the healing sessions – Betty's clairvoyance was astounding. She told Shirley and myself in graphic detail about people in our lives, past and present; and when given just a name she came up with character assessments of incredible accuracy.

I now see Betty less frequently but the phenomena continue. During a recent session she said she had a message for me. She had been asked to sit back while her spirits took over the healing. I was to close my eyes and relax completely.

After about a minute I felt as though my whole body was plugged into the mains, such was the surge of current from my head to my toes. I opened my eyes momentarily to see that Betty was not even touching me. As usual Shirley was sitting in the room as an observer while Betty sat at the bottom of the couch poised on her chair. I closed my eyes again and it felt as though I was experiencing some form of levitation – a strange, floating feeling.

I opened my eyes as Betty spoke and broke the silence, the room appeared to be a bright yellow, the colour of daffodils. I was frightened – what had happened? Betty remarked on the colour, I was not imagining it. The yellow colour eventually faded but later the ceiling turned a beautiful shade of blue, and this time the phenomenon was witnessed by all three of us. Betty said these were the colours of healing.

Often I would leave with my hair literally standing on end, such was the power Betty generated in the healing room.

After the click in his spine Peter was able, for the first time in his life, to lie down all night without being crippled with pain. (From birth he had a crack in his spine and had never been able to lie down – never mind sleep – for more than two hours at a time. This was in part an inherited illness. His sister had been born with *spina bifida* and died of it at an early age.)

You will have noticed how, during one of Peter's last sessions, the room seemed to turn bright yellow and then blue, and that I said these were the colours of healing. Colour does indeed play an important part in the healing process – hospital wards, as you will certainly have observed, are usually painted some pale restful colour, usually green, never, say, a vivid red. If you want to explore this topic, I can recommend an excellent book, *The Healing Power of Crystals* by Magda Palmer, which explores the subject in more depth.

The book explains that some six thousand years ago the ancient Sumerians hit upon a system of colour connections between Earth and the other planets, with appropriate stones for each. Thus green pearls were right for Venus, rose and scarlet stones for Mars; and so on. The book further points out that traditional lore suggests a link between colours and the energy points of the body (that is, the vortices), with one day of the week, and one or two particular stones, specially designated for each. Thus green is the colour for troubles of the heart, with Monday the best day and dioptase or malachite the best stones. Red is for ailments connected with the base of the spine, with Tuesday the preferred day and fire opal or red spinel the best minerals. As Magda Palmer says, we all know the pleasure that colour can bring to our souls, through the glories of nature or painting. Do we also realize the benefits it can bring to our bodies?

Colour healing is a very easy way to self-healing. We use colour every day of our lives – in clothes, curtains, furniture, carpets and so on. Out of doors, in spring and summer especially, there are the natural colours of grass, trees, flowers, shrubs, hedgerows and, of course, clouds and sky. Especially uplifting in England is a bright blue sky – it automatically makes you feel better.

Colour rays link up with the colour or colours that you are wearing. For instance if a female patient is wearing green and blue I can see green and blue rays shining down on her. There will be a few other colours as well, but the predominant ones will be green or blue. Black is often a smart colour to wear, but it will repel the energy rays. That is why black has been traditionally worn in Latin countries – it keeps you cool because it repels the sun's rays. The rays attracted will be very negative, with a preponderance of greys and browns. To correct this, wear accessories such as a bright pocket handkerchief or a brightly coloured scarf. These will attract energy colours.

All this has a bearing on health, so choose your colours carefully. In a moment I will tell you how.

The study of colours in healing has fascinated me over many years. It is exciting and ever-changing. One day I was treating a lady for an arthritic complaint. She was wearing beige at the time, and yet I saw a bright pinky-red ray shining down on her. I told her what I could see and she immediately said, 'Don't laugh, but that is the colour of the underwear I have got on today.' So you see, it doesn't matter whether the colour is visible or not; it will still attract the ray.

My patients are able to see for themselves all the colours of the rainbow. While I am topping them up, their mind energy expands and they are able to see into the energy dimension. You will do so as well when you are carrying out the exercises in this book, and especially as you become more proficient at partly leaving the body. Another bonus!

Attracting the rays for self-healing is a very easy exercise. Everyone can do it, at whatever stage of spiritual development, and it will bring great joy.

COLOUR EXERCISE

Sit or lie down. Breathe deeply three times, and feel the whole of your body relaxing. You will also feel peaceful. If you have problems relaxing, don't worry. Just go straight into the exercise.

Think outwards toward the universe – you have had a lot of practice already – but don't put any effort into it. The less you force yourself, the faster you will travel! Now ask for the coloured ray you need most, and wait. You will suddenly see a colour in your mind's eye, perhaps many colours. But make no mistake, the spirit colour therapists are usually bang on when it comes to the colour or colours you most need. As your colours become clearer and brighter don't do any more work yourself, just revel in the healing that you are receiving. The rays are perpetually vibrating throughout the universe.

In this dimension the beauty is hidden from us most of the time because of the dense atmosphere. I have seen colours on my astral travels so beautiful they appear to be shot with gold and silver threads – an almost incredible enhancement and one impossible to describe with mere words. These rays are powerful energies that can flow through matter, as of course does all energy.

Colour is a cosmic force and is essentially spiritual. Dis-ease in the energy counterpart cannot continue when it is regularly permeated by the rays, nor indeed can that in the physical body. The more you practise colour healing, the healthier you will be.

If you want to attract the colour you feel you need, then choose your wardrobe accordingly.

RED   The colour for energy. Breaks up arthritic crystal, releases negative energies within the body, helps the circulation and combats blood deficiency diseases. To aid your visualization technique, think of blood!

ORANGE   Wonderful for people suffering from asthma, fear, depression, and lethargy. Easy to visualize – just think of an orange!

YELLOW   Most definitely, the colour for use when meditating. Very spiritual, it brings love and peace into your home and life. It is a purifying ray. To help your visualization, think of a daffodil.

GREEN   The colour for the nervous system, and especially good for muscle spasms. It is soothing – after all it is nature's colour! Choose a shade you feel happy with, for that will be the best one for you. To help you at the start, visualize grass.

BLUE   The healing ray. This is the colour that is always seen when healing is taking place. It calms both the positive and negative electromagnetic links around the body. Excellent for combating epilepsy, depression, fevers and inflammation, it is the healing ray *par excellence*. It eases all dis-ease.

VIOLET   The colour for the nervous system, fatigue and emotional problems. Think of violets. Use the blue ray to finish off.

AMETHYST   An excellent cure for insomnia. If you can, find an amethyst stone of beautiful, pale bluish-violet and keep it under your pillow.

PINK   I have left this till last because I have never used it without red, it doesn't seem to do very much on its own. If your experience is different to mine and you have had success with this colour, please let me know.

An easy and pleasant way of making sure that you always have the right colour somewhere around your dress is to buy a selection of silk or nylon scarves or handkerchiefs. You can also try beaming colours to friends who need help. Remember, the thought is the deed. Colours can constitute your absent healing chart. They are certainly good for healing at a distance.

As John Ruskin wrote: 'The purest and most thoughtful minds are those which love colour the most.' So good luck with this method. I know you will feel all the better for having tried it.

The control tower of the whole body is mind energy. The brain is the computer; mind energy the power that activates it. Without the mind energy the brain and the physical body die.

Plato saw man as a trinity of soul, soul body, and earth body. I see the mind as the soul, the energy counterpart as the soul body, and the physical body as the earth body. Plato lived more than two thousand years ago; I started studying the subject a mere sixteen years ago, yet came up with the same thought and did not read Plato until after I had done so. If our theory is a load of bunkum, then how has it survived? And how has it survived if there is no contact between mind and mind? There is also the fact that all yogic exercises, themselves hundreds of years old, are based on the energy counterpart with its vortices and meridian lines. My own interest began when I actually saw these things. Believe me, if they did not exist, then neither should we.

To end this chapter, I would like you to do an exercise in which once again you will manipulate mind energy through the use of the imagination. It will take you a little further along the path than the exercises so far. This time we add a little discipline.

Choose a quiet room, sit down and relax. Breathe deeply. Perhaps you would like to play some soothing background music. Once you feel peaceful, close your eyes. Now picture a halo around your head, a bright white halo. Now watch it expanding outwards *ad infinitum*. Now hold it. (This is where the discipline comes in). When you have held it in position for a few seconds, let it go, then watch it reducing in size until it looks like a normal halo again.

Do this exercise three times or more, until you have the feeling that you and you only are in control. By holding the mind energy you will experience a feeling of power, a feeling that *you* will control your life.

This is the first step in mind control through discipline. You can take the pressure off your brain and body at will, and yet you will hardly notice you are doing so because the feeling of relaxation is total.

Harnessing mind energy is fascinating and it is fun.

In the next chapter you will find exercises that will take you further along your own journey of enlightenment.

Three

ANALYSIS THROUGH EXERCISES

Trust one who has gone through it.

Virgil (70–19 B.C.)

The following exercises are the next steps that you will take in expanding your mind by activating your imagination. The first one is important in rooting you firmly to earth. The second and third will lift you from the earth up into the sky. The fourth will secure you a few moments of peace and privacy when you are hassled and besieged by other people.

BACK TO YOUR ROOTS

To prepare for the first three exercises I want you to choose a time when you know you will be alone, unplug the telephone or take it off the hook, lock all doors and choose a comfortable chair. (By the way, if family or other domestic circumstances make this difficult, there is one small private room in the house which will nicely fulfil all these conditions!)

Now, make sure that you are comfortable and warm, and when you are feeling cosy and happy, close your eyes. Breathe deeply three times.

Now I want you to imagine lovely fibrous roots

49

going down into the earth. Feel yourself being pulled down into your chair as the roots grow downwards into the very centre of the earth. *Feel* those roots as they cling to the earth's rich soil. Take your time. There is no hurry. As you identify with the deeply burrowing roots, you will experience a wonderful feeling of security, of being a part of this planet, of simple belonging. Now visualize the fibrous roots thickening until they take on the appearance of tubers. When you can 'see' or 'know' that this has happened, you will be earthed.

Now I am going to ask you to put to yourself two questions which will test how you got on.

1. Did you have a problem seeing the roots as they went down, or knowing that they were doing so? If you did, you are too easily swayed by others, too eager to listen and be carried away by their views.

2. If you had no problem simply watching the roots go down, did you nevertheless find it difficult to persevere and watch them strengthen into tubers? If so, you lack perseverance. You soon get bored with the realities of life, which is the opposite vice to letting reality get on top of you. Therefore you will need to strengthen your own roots before soaring away into the sky. You cannot fly until you are earthed; otherwise, when the moment arrives to 'come down to earth', you will do so with a nasty bump. I have met many mediums and healers who were not earthed – all people who

should have known better. They wafted away on
cloud nine with undisciplined mind energy, no roots
and no direction, and as a result their forecasts
and diagnoses were unbelievably stupid. Yet most
of them had talent and with careful earthing this
could have been used. How sad for them and for
the rest of us!

LIFT OFF

Now for the second exercise. Once again I am going
to ask you to sit quietly and close your eyes. Breathe
deeply three times. (You are going to do a lot of this,
so you might as well get used to it!) I want you to
summon up a picture of a field and in that field to
visualize an air balloon. Don't strain, but focus your
attention on the field. How big is it? Are there trees
and if so what sort are they? Is there water around
– maybe a pond with ducks and moorhens on it?
Or perhaps there are just ditches. Are there cows or
sheep in the field? And so on. Let your mind's eye
travel freely around, observing all these things. This
first stage is vital to the whole exercise because as
you let your imagination play, so your mind energy
is expanding outwards, linking up with cosmic forces
which will have the effect of feeding back to it more
strength. Remember too that it is your field and
nobody else's! You can see in it what you will.

Now bring your attention to bear on the balloon
and the basket attached beneath it. Will you need
some steps or a stool to enable you to climb into

the basket? If so, put them in place. What colour is the balloon? Look at it carefully and colours will appear. But now you may find you are straining a bit too hard and feeling tension in your shoulders. If so, relax. Breathe deeply three more times. When you have done this, step into the basket. Are there things in it? Note them, if there are. Then settle down comfortably on the seat if there is one. If there is not, then mentally create a chair.

Now imagine the balloon lifting off and savour the sensation of this. Perhaps the ascent will be a little unsteady at the beginning or perhaps it will be quick and straight. Feel the wind on your face, feel the comforting warmth of the sun on your body.

Now look over the side of the basket. There beneath you is the countryside as you have never seen it before. Trees, animals, houses begin to take on an oddly toy-like look. The roads streak like thin ribbons through the villages and fields.

Up and up! Now you are really away and the earth beneath you seems to lose significance as it recedes. There is total peace around you in the clear air and now you start feeling a part of the universe and at one with it. Relax in the warm sun and take in the energy of this wonderful new world which will stimulate and revitalize you.

Healing energies are all around you. Perhaps you will see their beautiful colours as your own mind energy links up with them. In any case your body will absorb them like a sponge. Feel it doing so! And now, ask for help for any problem you may have, whether physical or emotional, and be absolutely confident that someone is listening and that help is at last at hand. Having assured yourself of this (and take plenty of time), think yourself down and return gently to earth.

As you descend, you will feel yourself getting heavier. Once more the roads, houses, trees and fields become distinct. Ease yourself slowly down into the field from which your journey began and, once down, look around it. Has it changed? Maybe a car has been parked in it since you began your ascent and is now waiting to take you home — for remember this is still the realm of the creative imagination.

That is the exercise. It can be practised again and again. Indeed it will have to be practised again and again, for the first time you try it you will almost certainly find that it is rather less easy than it sounds. Here are some questions and comments to enable you to gauge your progress.

1. Did you start on the initial preparations, longing for peace of mind, then decide that the whole thing was more trouble than it was worth and give up? If so, your mind energy was negative, funnelled in and pressing down on the brain as already described, causing dysfunction of the electro-magnetic circuit around your body and producing depression and fatigue. Don't worry! Next time, be a bit tougher with yourself. Force yourself to carry on. You have a lifetime to change in, so what's the hurry?

2. Perhaps you completed the preparations stage but once in the basket, warm and comfortable and with closed eyes, found yourself unable to 'see' anything. Again, don't worry, this is quite normal at the beginner's stage. Just feel total confidence in the progress you have made so far and little by little pictures will start to appear. This is because you are stimulating the mind energy which, as it expands, links up with outside forces which feed back to it increased power and give your mind a helping hand. Moreover if you cannot see when you first start doing this exercise, you can almost certainly feel. One thing leads to another!

3. But if you *can* see, let me help you interpret the messages. The field you saw, was it almost bare of trees and hedges? In that case, you wish to lead as uncluttered a life as possible with the minimum of hangers-on. That sounds a bit selfish and perhaps that is what you are, but who isn't sometimes? As you repeat the exercise you may find yourself adding a tree or two and so be able, back in the everyday world, to tolerate a few more people in your life and even be able to help them. This, however, will be a gradual change. The lasting changes in our lives almost always come slowly and overnight conversions are suspect. If by contrast your field is over-cluttered, then you cannot see the wood for the trees and your life is over-complicated and overcrowded and needs simplifying. If, as you continue to repeat the exercise, the trees in your field

thin out, you can be confident that this is indeed the direction in which you are moving.

I hope by now you are beginning to see what this exercise is meant to be doing for you. Its purpose is mind expansion, the improvement of your own life and the monitoring of your own progress by the linking of your own mind energies to the Universal Mind.

4. What were the colours and patterns of your balloon? Check the colour chart in the previous chapter for your own diagnosis. Remember, whatever you need you will attract. If your balloon is a mixture of colours, then congratulate yourself. You are a beautiful balance of the physical and the spiritual. But again, you can monitor your progress every time you do the exercise.

5. What did you find in the basket when you climbed into it? Was it cluttered or uncluttered? Whichever it was, you are now in a position to interpret its state for yourself.

6. When it came to the ascent, did you find take-off difficult? If so, you are afraid of change. You want to feel safe but all you are really doing is imprisoning yourself both physically and spiritually, because where there is fear there can be no freedom, whether of thought, word or deed. Don't worry, 90 per cent of us are cowards at heart. Join the club, as they

say. What is important is that you should persevere in your efforts to change. And, you *can* change, I promise you. But perhaps you went to the opposite extreme and your balloon shot up with alarming speed. In that case, in your everyday life, you are trying to go too fast too soon and failing to attend to detail. Again, with practice, as you continue to repeat this exercise, you will get your balloon to ascend at a more sensible rate and in consequence will find, for the first time in your life perhaps, that back in the everyday world you are noticing all sorts of apparently unimportant things and becoming aware of the emotions of other people.

7. Were you brave enough to look over the side of the basket or did you sit tight? If the latter, you are evidently uninterested in anything except your personal concerns. You are probably also afraid. If, however, you found yourself looking over the side, then you are keenly interested in everything around you, in all the life of the world. Congratulations again! You will not find it difficult to grasp what I have been talking about and to set about your problems accordingly.

8. When you were finally aloft, up there away from the humdrum world and at one with the universe, how did you feel? Did you feel peaceful, or nervous and even afraid? Your answer will show whether the healing powers of the exercise were working on you or not.

9. Did you find it difficult to ask for help? Perhaps you cannot believe that there is anyone out there listening. Let me assure you that given the opportunity your mind energy could be in touch with the Universal Mind permanently.

10. Did you return to earth with a thud, or gently? If the former, then you were not in control of your mind energy. If the latter, then you are beginning to work along with it.

11. When you returned to earth, did you find that your field had changed in appearance at all – more trees, fewer trees, whatever? If so, then you had begun to make progress in modifying your attitudes even during your first trip. This is great news – provided the progress was in the right direction, of course!

12. When you landed, did you visualize a car waiting in or by the side of the field to take you home? The answer to this one tells you a lot about yourself. The presence of a car suggests that you still have childish attitudes – you want a sweetie for being good. If, however, you are not bothered about transport, that is a sign of independence.

But of course this last comment must not be misunderstood. All mature, well-balanced people have many elements in their make-up. All of us have both a male and a female side and if either is repressed too violently the whole character is thrown out of true. Similarly 'the child is father to the man' and must remain in him to the end of his days. Especially as the child is the source of our imagination. Children have open minds and incredible imaginations, until this is suppressed in the interests of 'reality'. As 'reality' moves in, psychic ability is driven out. That is why so many children become difficult to manage. They, like adults, need their dreams. For after all, what *is* reality? It is worthless except when shaped by imagination just as matter is worthless except when shaped by mind.

So what I am saying is, activate your imagination. That was the guiding idea behind the exercise which you have just read. Each change you make in the pictures you see when repeating it will modify your actions, your attitudes and the rest of your day-to-day life as you return to it when the experience is over.

Now do you see what imagination is all about? This exercise is also teaching you to discipline your mind so that you will eventually have total control over your spiritual and psychic health and happiness.

Now here comes a third exercise. The first two were basic, vital to your progress, but perhaps also a little severe – what used to be called character-building. This one puts the main emphasis on enjoyment – for after all, what are our lives for if not to be enjoyed? It will, however, be no less valuable than the first two in giving you practice in expanding your imagination and in teaching you about yourself.

UP IN THE CLOUDS

As before, sit down quietly and close your eyes. Breathe deeply three times. Now feel yourself floating peacefully out of the window. You really can imagine this in more than a fanciful sense because once more it is the mind that is doing the work in all this and mind is energy and can pass through anything. Now you are outside and can feel yourself lift off and leave the ground, slowly at first, then gradually picking up speed. I'm sure there's a bit of Mary Poppins in all of us!

Above you are clouds. Soon you will reach them and as you do so jump on the one which you like the best and which you think will be the most comfortable. Make yourself at home on it. You can lie on your back looking up at the sky above, or lean over and look down at the earth. You will feel free and relaxed but most of all you will be at peace.

Feel the buoyancy of the cloud and its texture. Perhaps it feels like cotton wool or perhaps it is more like a beautiful piece of silk. Whatever it feels like, enjoy it. You are drifting along. If you are looking up, what do you see? Perhaps more clouds or perhaps a blue sky or perhaps it is night and you are able to study the stars. Concentrate so that you can remember every detail.

If you are lying down, what can you see as you look over the edge? Fields, towns, villages, highways, forests, rivers, lakes, mountains, churches, beacons. Whatever the sights below you, remember them.

Now continue to enjoy the total peace. Breathe deeply three times. If you want your cloud to go higher, just think yourself up and up. Travel is unlimited; there are no barriers. Stay aloft on your cloud for as long as you wish. When you feel it is time to return, just think yourself down. Your cloud, when it reaches the earth, will evaporate into mist and disappear.

Now, as before, let us go through your experience.

1. Did you find lift-off difficult? If you did, you have obviously become frightened of change. But don't worry. When practising this exercise for the first few times, just skip this lift-off part and visualize yourself on the cloud. But don't skip it too often!

2. If you found lift-off easy but failed to pick up speed, this means you are cautious but still willing to have a go, so again, don't worry.

3. If, however, you went zooming away rather too fast, then you are so eager for change and excitement that you could land yourself in trouble. The best take-off starts slowly but gradually builds up speed. As you continue to practise the exercise, always strive for this middle path and little by little it will balance your personality.

4. What did your cloud look like? Was it small, big, elongated, wide or middling? If it was small, you expect very little from life and perhaps are afraid to ask for anything more. If it was big, you embrace life with open arms and expect as much love from other people as you give out. If it is elongated, you want more than your fair share and if it is fat the same thing goes. If it is middling, you are a moderate personality and perhaps also a bit staid. Why not break out now and then?

5. Did you lie on your back looking up? If you did, were there clouds above you, a blue sky, or was it night? If it was night were there stars? If there were clouds, your life is a bit hazy and this applies especially to your ideas about the future. Try to melt them away and gain more clarity of vision. A blue sky, however, is a happier indication. It suggests you have a clear idea of what you want from your life and would like to go out and get it. Why not! If it was night there is a darker side involved. You have a secretive nature and want to keep things to yourself – that is, if the night was starless. But if there were stars you have an affinity with the universe.

6. Were you lying down? What did you see below? If you saw open fields with few trees in them and few houses around, then your life at the moment is barren. At your next attempt, try to visualize more detail. If you saw forests, then your life is over-complicated. Try to thin out the trees. Or did

you see lakes and mountains or a landscape with a beautiful river flowing through? Water is always an excellent thing to see, for it is spiritual and fluid like our energy bodies and our minds. Mountains also have a mystical significance, forever reaching up from the earth.

7. Did you want to go higher? If so, you are eager to investigate and break down barriers.

All these exercises will probably reveal you as a mixture of opposing attitudes. Most people are. But all of them will help you to analyse yourself and to solve your problems as you practise them. You will be surprised how easy they make it to work things out.

But back in the rough-and-tumble world of every day you are probably besieged not only by problems but by people. Here is a short exercise to give you protection when others become too demanding.

THE AURIC EGG

This exercise is a 'quickie' and can even be practised standing up. Close your eyes, then summon up the image of a huge egg. It will have a door in it. Walk through the door and lock it. Inside you will find masses of enormous cushions. Flop down on to them and when you are feeling completely relaxed begin to harden the eggshell until it is like rock or iron. Yes, harden the door too! When you are satisfied that it can in no way be broken into, relax and carry on with the ordinary affairs of your day.

This exercise is particularly beneficial if your life is such as to require you to listen constantly to other people's problems, for the danger of this is that you will absorb their aura or mind energy into your own. It is not meant to make you selfish, however. Whenever you feel that sympathy and compassion are called for, just walk back through the door. But when you see someone approaching whom you do not wish to meet or someone arrives who you know spells trouble, jump into your egg for a few seconds. It will work wonders!

I suggest that when you first try these exercises you have a friend reading from the book to guide you. With practice you will remember them.

CONCLUSION

Know that all these exercises are linking you up with the tidal waves of energy that move the living sea of the universe. Through doing them you are becoming a part of this whole. Feel it. Feel the subtle changes in your body as it leaves the pull of the earth and releases itself from the bonds that tie us to its troubles and cares. You will return, but on your own terms and with the knowledge that you can leave again at will.

Never again will you be a prisoner of gravity. You will become a free spirit. You will have freedom of thought, word and deed, an instinctive knowledge of right and wrong. You will want to simplify your life so that you will have more time to spend on the things that really matter: love, family and friends, and perhaps also to teach others what you have learned so that they may share your spiritual knowledge. You will also find yourself carried away on a wave of audible silence – an experience you will never forget!

By carrying out these exercises you have begun the vital process of expanding your mind energy through controlled use of the imagination. Now I am going to take you one important step further. I am going to show you how imagination and mind energy are the basis of the art of spiritual healing – and, in the first instance, of self-healing.

Four

SELF-HEALING

It seldom happens that a man changes his life through his habitual reasoning. No matter how fully he may sense the new plans and aims revealed to him by reason, he continues to plod along in the old paths until his life becomes frustrating and unbearable – he finally makes the change only when his usual life can no longer be tolerated.

Tolstoy (1828–1910)

We come into this life alone and we leave it alone. In between we are helped first by parents, then by teachers, and meanwhile, hopefully, we begin to help ourselves.

Unfortunately, we have also acquired dependency, and in the matter of healing we find it very difficult to break away from the medical profession and help ourselves. From the time we are babes in arms everything is done for us; that is why, for most children, school comes as a shock. Teachers make children think for themselves – or should do. The children whose parents have encouraged them from an early age to do things for themselves are usually way ahead of those who haven't, quite a few of whom remain dependent throughout their school years.

How can you help your child even before he or

she starts to communicate? I am going to take you through the next exercise as though I were teaching a child. We will come to the more adult bit later, but if you stay with the first part it will be of immense value and help to you and your children in putting your roots down, so to speak.

A CHILD'S FIRST STEPS

A child has grazed its knee and is crying. It comes to me for help. I sit it on a chair, get some cotton wool and bathe the wound with warm water with a little antiseptic in it. I then place my hand, clean of course, over the graze but not touching it, and hold it there for a few seconds. Then I take the child's hand and put it over the graze, repeating the words, 'Heal yourself'. It doesn't matter at all if the child is still crying and has no intention of doing any such thing: just keep repeating, 'Heal yourself'. From an early age you are giving the responsibility of this to the child.

If a child has a headache I do the same sort of thing. I sit it on my knee and put my hand to its head. Then I take the child's hand and place it under mine, repeating 'Heal yourself'. These words will eventually become part of the child's experience and will be totally accepted as he or she matures.

When the child is a little older, say about the age of five, you can add another exercise. Ask it to close its eyes and pretend it has a bowl of cotton wool and a basin of warm water on a table in front of it. Ask it to pretend to dip the cotton wool in the water and clean the wound, then to wipe it with an imaginary clean cloth and put on a plaster. All these operations take place in the child's imagination. What is happening to the child's mind while it is carrying them out?

First of all, the mind energy is expanding. The actions have become a game and the child is releasing from the brain its own endorphins, which are natural painkillers. A child's imagination is very easily stimulated. It will find its fun in the visualization which will eventually become easy. As it goes through the process of cleansing and the rest, the pressure of mind energy is taken off the brain and body and opens up the energy vortices and meridian lines, which in turn enable the child to draw in more life force. Thus the healing process begins. Instead of concentrating negativity on the wound the child will have a positive attitude and the feeling that he or she is in control.

Don't worry if your child doesn't respond immediately. Play games with it every now and then when it is well, then when it is ill, or merely grazed or bruised, it will find it that much easier to put the play into practice.

Parents are always saying to their children, 'Let me kiss it and make it better.' It would be just as easy to say, 'You make it better and this is how we will do it.' Join in the fun, for that is what it is. The younger the child, the more independent it will become, and as it grows up, it will not think it right to leave you, the parent, with all the responsibility.

Now we move on to the adult exercises. But before we get down to the brass tacks of self-healing, here is one I would like you to do to relax you and stimulate your imagination.

A LAZE ON THE BEACH

Sit quietly, close your eyes and breathe deeply three times. Then imagine that you are standing on the top of a cliff looking out to the sea. The day has been warm and balmy. Now the sun is beginning to set and its beautiful gold-orange glow is shimmering on the water.

Now I want you to take a walk along the top of the cliff drinking in all the beauty. Eventually you will come to a flight of wooden steps leading down the cliffside. Walk down these steps, counting them as you go. There are twenty in all. When you get to the bottom you will see, near the sea's edge, a rock with a flat surface. Sit on this rock and look out over the sea. Now, once again, breathe deeply three times and repeat the following words: 'I feel relaxed, happy and healthy. This is how I want to feel for the rest of my life. This is how I *will* feel from now onwards, all the time.'

After a while stand up, open your arms, and shout your good news to the world: 'I feel so well!' Then climb back up the wooden steps, counting as you go, and when you reach the top walk back to the spot from which you imagined yourself setting off. By now the sun will have set but say to yourself: 'When it rises in the morning my whole life will have changed.'

What will this exercise have done for you? First of all, as you looked at the imaginary sunset, your mind energy will have been projected out and away from your body. Secondly, the scene will have relaxed you by bringing into action your appreciation of colour and beauty. The walk itself will also have been relaxing and stimulating and will have opened up a whole new energy field. When you walked down the steps you will have entered your subconscious being, where negative congestive energies were waiting to be released. Self-hypnosis, in fact.

Remember at all times – you, and you alone, are in control; nobody else. When you reached the bottom of the cliff and sat on the rock looking out towards the sea, you were mentally in a position to give yourself auto-suggestion, with thoughts that would stay in the lower levels of your mind energy. In this stage you can suggest anything to yourself and this will stay with you long after you have forgotten it. You are, if you like, dictating on to a tape from which nothing can ever be wiped out unless you wish it to be. Climbing back up the steps will have the effect of drawing the mind energy back into your body where it will settle itself into position, and as you walk back to the point from which you started you should be feeling a new person.

Remember, this is *your* mind space. Don't allow anyone else in. It is safe and there is no way in which it can cause harm. What it will do is to give you an insight into your own capabilities and a place to which you can escape from problems and perhaps solve a few.

Tapes explaining the exercises are available (see end of book for details). So, if you find this exercise a bit hard to remember at first, you can listen to it on a tape. Or you could ask someone to read it out for you from this book. Soon you will get the hang of it and once you have gained confidence you can vary it a bit and do the things that relax you best. Imagination is the key. It will unlock the universe for you. And once you get the idea of what is happening to your mind energy, your vortices and your meridian lines, the whole exercise will become easier.

Now, if you are still relaxed, I should like to take you into the most important exercise of all.

THE MIND MEDICINE ROOM

Remember, you will be using this room for the rest of your life and it will give you health, happiness and independence. No longer will you visit your doctor for minor ailments, and when you do have to ask the medical profession for help you can hasten your own recovery. In the present state of orthodox medicine, with its endless delays and crippling costs, this is no small benefit.

Whatever you do, please don't skip any part

of this exercise because you are building it with mind energy and it will become a pharmacy in the energy dimension and cannot be destroyed. The power of this room will be extraordinary, and like any building it is the foundation that is the most important part.

So here is the exercise:

Once again, sit or lie down, close your eyes and *breathe deeply three times*. When you have done this, I want you to imagine a corridor. Walk along the corridor and soon you will find a door. Your name will be on the door and in the lock you will see a key. Open the door, take the key out of the lock, walk into the room, close the door and lock it from the inside.

Now look around you. This is your mind space. You will find the room furnished with shelves and benches and two windows overlooking parkland. There will also be an easy chair.

This is your pharmacy and your task from now on will be to stock it with whatever you need. So ask yourself what you need most at the present time. Do you get migraines? Are you a diabetic? Do you suffer from arthritis and spend much of your time in pain? Whatever it is, you will now take your first step towards curing it.

Let us assume you are suffering from a simple headache. Sit in the easy chair, close your eyes and picture a jar. Now write 'Headache Pills' on a label and stick it on the jar. Now look inside the jar. By your simple act of labelling, headache pills will have appeared in it, enough to last you a lifetime. So help yourself to two or three of them, put them in your mouth, suck or swallow them and place the jar on the bench. Sit quietly and your headache will go.

Impossible? Not so. But what have you actually done?

By projecting your mind toward the problem and knowing, without any doubt, you are going to be cured, you are releasing your own natural painkillers – endorphins, to be precise. Your mind is controlling the action of the body.

By keeping yourself occupied you have also taken a major step toward independence. Constructing this powerful pharmacy you can cure all your ills. It is a truly magical room.

Visit your Mind Medicine Room every day, whether you are ill or not. Add something every time you enter it. Write more labels to put on empty jars. It is much better to be prepared for any eventuality. One day, it may be a matter of great urgency.

There is no end to the list. Cotton wool, slimming pills, backache pills, hormone pills, heroin or other drugs for addicts. Yes! An addict needs a daily shot while trying to kick the habit. This way makes it a lot easier and can give the same stimulation, for whatever you believe is in the jars, so it will be. What you are building up are energy pills, energy syringes. And everything in energy does exist.

As another example, take the case of a diabetic. He or she walks into the Medicine Room, locks it, takes a syringe from its sterile package in the jar or box and enough insulin from its bottle to last a day. The needle will then be injected into the skin, the skin will be gently rubbed and the syringe thrown away. It will disappear, incidentally – all rubbish automatically disappears. The jar or box will then be returned to its place and the bottle also. The sufferer will now sit down quietly and relax.

A feeling of well-being and expectation will be experienced as soon as the insulin is injected. For the act of injecting it stimulates the energy system which, in turn, stimulates the pancreas. And so the cure begins. Many people find a spirit doctor waiting for them so they just sit down, close their eyes, and relax, while healing is taking place.

Visit your pharmacy for at least five minutes every day, whether you are well or ill. Over the months and years you will probably change things in it. Maybe you will change the benches and shelves and if you are a woman you will want prettier bottles and even some dramatic potions! Time spent in the pharmacy when you are well will speed the cure when you are ill. With this exercise you are building energy, which is power. Its results will change your life.

Another way of keeping healthy is to think positively at all times. No-one in the world can achieve this but if you think you can you will probably be positive 50 per cent of the time. Negativity is a killer. Yes! we do need the balance. How else would we know how great it feels to be positive if we are never negative? We need the balance – though wouldn't it be nice (nice but difficult, of course), if we could achieve a ratio of 70 per cent positive, 30 per cent negative? At the moment there are so many people who exhibit this ratio in reverse! Negativity is becoming a disease in itself.

What is the first step? Limit yourself to five minutes negative thought – then switch off. This is extremely difficult but something you have to do, for unless you do it your thought processes will control you, and not the other way round. With a disciplined mind, *you* are in control.

Now for mind discipline of a quite different sort – that which I recommend for fighting tumours, malignant or benign.

The doctor pronounces the dreaded word 'Cancer' and the patient's life shatters, like a car windscreen shattered by a stone. It is a devastating moment, and all the worse when, as so often happens, it has to be borne alone. There follows the stunned departure from the hospital or surgery, the crossing of roads, the boarding of trains or buses – a most dangerous journey, for the victim is in mental agony, indeed, often suicidal. I personally know of two cases where the person on whom this sentence of death had just been passed deliberately walked under a bus or car.

Many of the letters I receive are from people who have suffered this truly horrific experience.

'I have just been given a death sentence,' wrote one. 'I have lung cancer and the surgeon has told me I only have three months at the most.'

'I can't believe it!' wrote another. 'I felt so well

and yet after a check-up it appears that I have breast cancer. I am so frightened.'

The most terrible thing about both these letters is that all *hope* has been taken away. Rather like the witch doctor pointing the bone.

Yet there *is* hope – always.

I have known people who have cured themselves of terminal cancer with visualization and I believe this therapy should be available at centres throughout the country. Hope is life. Without it we kill ourselves.

Fortunately, there is something more powerful than cancer, and that is the mind. With your mind you can reverse the workings of your body and reduce any tumour to the condition of a trembling jelly. You can knock it for six with your aggression. Are you feeling angry that your body has turned on you? Then let it feel the full vent of your anger in return. Attack the tumour, or the white blood cells, with aggression. Don't give in, fight every inch of the way, and if you have to neglect your home, your family or your friends in order to do so, then so be it.

To deal with a tumour, malignant or benign, the following visualization exercise can be helpful. First, allow yourself about ten minutes of complete peace to prepare yourself for the fight ahead. Now sit down, make yourself comfortable, close your eyes and breathe deeply three times. When you have done this, imagine yourself in a garden. You are standing there in the middle of the lawn, you are wearing very loose clothes and sandals. The sun is coming up and you can feel the warmth penetrating the whole of your body, relaxing every muscle.

Now I want you to walk to the bottom of the lawn where you will find ten steps going down to a terrace. Descend the steps slowly and count them as you go: 1, 2, 3, 4, 5, 6, 7, 8, 9, 10. You reach the terrace and look out towards a landscape of mountains, forests and rivers. This is your mind space. It belongs only to you. It is safe and secure. Remember this. Now, once more, breathe deeply three times.

Then turn right and walk down the terrace, until you find six steps leading down to a smaller terrace. Count the steps as you go. To the right of the terrace is a pool. Remove your clothes and walk into it, sink down into the warm relaxing water, which is also a powerful energy source. As you relax, you will feel your body absorbing the energy and you will begin to feel rejuvenated but still peaceful. Enjoy the pool until you feel ready to leave it, then climb out of it, dry yourself off on the towel by the side of the pool and dress yourself again. Walk back up the six steps, counting as you go. Walk along the terrace and up the ten higher steps, counting again, and return to the spot on the lawn from which your journey began.

Now you are rejuvenated. Your energy fields have opened up. It is the moment to launch your attack. Make yourself comfortable, close your eyes, and visualize your tumour or tumours. You will find a quantity of small pellets in your hand. Insert them into the tumours and when you have done so watch the tumours explode and vanish. Do this exercise as many times a day as you like. Your mind is the most powerful ally you have. MENTAL ENERGY WORKS. Perhaps you can think up even more aggressive things to do. If so, do them. Your tumour won't know what's hit it. Don't give up. Ever.

If you have leukaemia practise a variant of this technique. Travel through the garden and bathe in the pool as before. Then, instead of pellets, equip yourself with a small vacuum cleaner and travel with it through your blood stream, sucking up all the cancerous and malignant cells and utterly destroying them. Alternatively, think up an imaginary substance which you can inject into yourself to destroy the excess white cells. Vary the weapons according to your own ideas but on no account despair if you cannot actually 'see' what you are doing. Just to know is enough. With practice all sorts of images will start to appear. Anything can happen, once you apply the power of your mind.

When you have finished your exercise, breathe deeply and imagine a blue healing liquid being poured into the top of your head. As it flows through your body it will take all the debris with it. You will then feel peaceful.

Repeat these exercises every day as many times as you wish. You are at war and there is no way you are going to retreat. Your body is going to do what you want it to do.

Becoming independent and controlling your own health is a wonderful feeling. No longer will you have that awful sense of dependency and being let down by those you trusted.

Above all, make up your mind that you will win. Don't have any doubts. I know you can do it because others have fought and won. Why not you?

The purpose of my work is to teach you this independence, this essential positivity.

As you become proficient in self-healing you will find that you have more confidence, you will be less likely to panic, because a visit to your Mind Medicine Room will calm you before fear has a chance to take you over. By strengthening your mind with exercises you will find it easier to control your physical body. This will give you a freedom that you will never have experienced before.

When you have become proficient at healing yourself you will be able to teach others. Life is for giving so please pass on your knowledge and new-found abilities.

The next chapter will add another dimension to your own structure.

Five

HEALING OTHERS

The success sometimes may come immediately but we must be ready to wait patiently even for what may look like an infinite length of time. The student who sets out with such a spirit of perseverance will surely find success and realization at last.

Vivekananda

Are you a healer? Your instinctive reply to this question is likely to be: 'I'm sure I'm not!' Well, don't be too sure! I certainly am not telling you that at your very first attempt you will be able to sense the energy counterpart projecting from someone else's body, as I described earlier, let alone truly visualize it complete with its vortices and meridian lines. Only psychics and sensitives can do this, as I have said, and they sometimes only after long practice. But here is a story to prove that most people really can heal, without any special knowledge, if they have two things: the will to do so, and the love.

The story concerns one of my patients, a young girl who worried so much about her mother that she became ill herself. She felt so inadequate, so powerless to help, that the negativity blocked her system. When she came to me for advice I told her the first thing she must do was to start thinking positively — that is, outwardly and away from herself. I told her to go home, place her hands on her mother's shoulders, think of my name and simply ask for help. After that she was to relax and let her mind become a blank.

The object of this was to remove all the negativity. Once she was calm, her energy would be free to flow out and her mother would not be prevented from receiving it. Moreover her own congested negativity would be released as the energy flowed, to the great benefit of them both!

She followed my instructions. Nothing happened at first, or, at least, so it appeared. But at the third attempt the girl experienced a delightful feeling of lightness and well-being and her mother said: 'I can feel my body tingling all over.' The mother had been suffering from an arthritic condition so bad it was threatening to cripple her. A few months later she was completely cured and her daughter had returned to being her usual happy and positive self.

If I tell you that already in your life you have probably healed at least one other person you may well not believe me, but in fact it is true. All you need is love, and a loving touch is the best start.

People touch and hug each other too little. They leave it till someone is dying, and then it's too late. Children, particularly, need to be brought up with this sort of love. Otherwise, how can they pass it on? Loving and hugging your child is the first and best means of keeping it happy and well and of curing it when it is ill. This seems obvious and of course most mothers do it as naturally as breathing. Some do not take to it so easily, perhaps. They are inhibited by upbringing, perhaps they are naturally selfish. But any loving is better than none and when a mother holds her sick child both of them benefit. If the mother is well her love will automatically open the system, life force will flow in abundance from her, and the child will continue to draw on it until it recovers. If the mother is sickly, she will draw life force from her child and this, in moderation, will do neither of them any harm. In fact, it will do them both good so long as the child has others around it – for instance a compassionate father, granny or aunt – from whom it can draw strength. This may seem a trifle complicated but really it is quite simple. We all draw from each other.

For some reason, touching is a cause of embarrassment for most people in Britain. Perhaps it is the climate, which makes us outwardly 'cold'. Perhaps it is connected with our system of education and our strange admiration for the 'stiff upper lip'. Certainly the Latin races, the Spanish, Italians and Greeks, suffer from no such inhibitions. They would think it most odd not to touch each other when happy, to glare at each other when annoyed, to hug, kiss, cry, according to their mood. So let us belatedly take a leaf out of their book and accept the simple fact that touching is therapeutic.

Touching is healing. It is a natural phenomenon. When the energy system is only working at half speed – that is, when the vortices are not spinning and drawing in life force as they should – then, when that sort of system is in contact with someone with a

81

vibrant energy system, it will draw off it. That is why one feels so much better in the company of vibrant people. By contrast, a 'jumping cracker' uses up his or her life force faster than it is drawn in. People of this sort draw from others but seldom give. That is why it is so exhausting to be around them for very long. I hope you are beginning to build up a picture of these two contrasting types – and have already decided which you would prefer to be!

Now imagine you are visiting a friend who has a bad headache – a common enough occurrence. Putting your arms around him or her, which is what you might like to do, would perhaps seem odd. So instead why not say: 'Let me put my hands on your head, the headache might go away.' And it almost certainly will. Most headaches are caused by tension. By the simple action of placing your hand on your friend's head, his or her depleted energy system will draw strength from yours, balance will be re-established and the cause of the tension removed. As you grow more experienced, something else will happen too. Sometimes your hands will become warm, even hot, as a result of the transfer of energy and the patient will feel an increased sense of well-being and peace as the transfer takes effect.

But of course there are people who refuse to be touched at all. What do you do then? The answer is simple. Sit quietly and expand your mind energy with the air balloon exercise described in chapter Three. While you are doing this you will be filling the house or room with life force at the same time as releasing your own tensions. If anyone in the house needs healing, his or her energy counterpart will absorb your energy like a sponge. This action will be quite unconscious on the sufferer's part. But the feeling of well-being and peace will be very real.

Another way to heal and release congestion in a sufferer's body is to use the hand as a magnet, working on the aura which, as I have already explained, protrudes about one and a half inches outside and around the physical body. Ask the sufferer to indicate to you exactly where the pain or discomfort is being felt, then place your hand directly over the spot and within approximately an inch of the skin. It doesn't matter whether you can actually feel anything. Most likely you will not. Simply start pulling your hand away from the spot, then back again, then away again, and continue to do this until the patient feels more comfortable. What you are actually doing is curing the congestion by pulling out the negative energy which illness always sucks in. Your action will relieve the pressure, allow the blood to circulate and rejuvenate the major organs which will vibrate again as they should. For minor ills at least, this method is invaluable.

If the patient has eye problems, try the laser beam technique. Imagine a fine laser beam or, if your scientific knowledge isn't quite up to this, picture a rod of energy and direct it towards the patient's eyes. This, too, is extremely effective.

Another method is to sit down with the patient and visualize a column of blue energy surrounding him or her. Watch the patient's body absorbing this energy. It will do so like a sponge. When the whole column of energy has been absorbed, replace it and repeat the process. This technique can be particularly helpful if the person you wish to heal refuses to co-operate. It can also be used as a method of absent healing, to be described in the next chapter.

What if the person is a long way away, perhaps abroad? All you have to do is sit quietly, think of that person, ask for help or simply think of a well-known healer, and you will automatically link into the healing network. Remember, the thought is the deed. Part of your mind energy, your life force, will be reaching that person before you have even finished thinking of the name! It is also a positive act on your part and by thinking loving thoughts towards someone else and by thinking outwards, your mind energy will expand and link up with universal energies. Whatever you give out will be returned tenfold or more.

If you could see the energy system as I can then you would see dull auras, medium auras, and very bright auras that would look like a sea of energy linking into each other, especially in a crowd. Mind energies, in particular, are always latching on to each other. That is why we very often know, instinctively, whether someone likes us or not. We are all part of each other. There is no way we can isolate ourselves. That is why it is important to surround yourself with loving family and friends. We can all do without people who are permanently aggressive, and if it is impossible for you to isolate yourself from them, then at least you must protect yourself. Practising the Auric Egg exercise, already described, is an excellent way of doing this.

Now here is the most basic healing experiment in the world. Try it out and see what happens. First, you must ask a friend or member of your family to stand facing you quietly in some convenient room. Now raise your hands and place them together at the top of his or her head, not touching it but about an inch and a half away. Now run your hands slowly and carefully down either side towards the ears and neck, keeping about the same distance from the skin. Then proceed on down towards the arms and so on towards the hands.

If you do this you will find areas of heat of which you become faintly aware. When you reach such an area start making gentle gestures outwards with one or both of your hands as though you were using a sort of magic magnet to extract a length of wool or string from that part of the other person's body. Flip this imaginary substance away as though discarding it. When you have finished, and if you start the initial exploratory movement again, you will find that the heat has disappeared. With it will have vanished whatever slight discomfort – a headache, say, or a minor ache in the arm – from which your 'patient' was suffering.

Like any other activity, this exercise takes a bit of practice. You may need to repeat it two or three times on different and separate occasions before you have reached the degree of mind sensitivity which is needed before you can feel these variations in temperature. But you *will* feel them. This is real healing, of however modest a kind, and the person on whom you are practising will benefit from it.

Please note that in teaching you the basic methods of psychic healing I am not suggesting that you should cold-shoulder your local GP or deprive yourself, when you need them, of the undoubted benefits of modern medical science. What I do believe is that there is much that we can do for ourselves. The methods I am teaching you are true 'alternative medicine'. They will help you to be independent – which is a thousand times better than dependency of any sort! They will also cut down the time you have to spend sitting in doctors' waiting rooms picking up viruses and colds! Many GPs agree with me here. In fact, they often send me patients and recommend my work! So why not start a small healing group with friends? We all need this sort of help.

There is also much scope for such groups among the disabled. If you are an invalid or confined to a wheelchair, please do not think healing others is not for you. The very reverse is the case. A paraplegic, for instance, cannot get out and take exercise. But for precisely that reason he will be filled with excess energy, and what the body does not need can be used for healing others. Allowing other people to draw off your energy will strengthen, not weaken, you. So an invalid's vortices will start spinning again because of the healing he or she has been giving to others and the whole body will feel more vibrant. I should like to see healing groups in every hospital in the land. Gestures of love can be embarrassing in a hospital, as they can outside it. But what could be less embarrassing than the sight of patients laying hands on each other in a compassionate and loving way?

Finally never forget, as you take your first steps in healing others, that while you are providing the energy it is the patient who is drawing it in, usually quietly, sometimes with difficulty, and quite often unconsciously. So many would-be healers think they have to push energy into the patient. That is quite wrong. Energy is not put into the patient. It is drawn from another energy system. Simply put your hands on the patient and he or she will draw energy from you. While this is happening your hands will probably become extremely warm, even hot, and your patient will feel a sense of well-being and peace as his or her system is rejuvenated. You will feel rejuvenated as well.

When a patient is really ill, with vortices almost grinding to a halt and meridian lines blocked, he or she will be able to draw in very little energy at the first attempt. But after a few days what energy has been drawn in will set the vortices spinning again at increased speed so that more and more energy will be drawn from the healer at the sessions that follow.

Whenever I heal someone, if I have been feeling tired at the beginning of the session, I always end up feeling on top of the world. This is because, as the energy is drawn out from you, so you take more life force in. Imagine an inexhaustible fluid energy. This is what is flowing from you to the patient, and from the cosmos to you.

All this is important to remember because otherwise you may become downcast if you fail to get a quick response. If you are going to try to heal others – and almost everyone can – forget about miracle healing. Unless you are a powerful professional healer, 'miracles' are rare.

What is important, no matter what the circumstances, is that love and compassion shall be present. It will be in your power to make another human being feel loved, comforted and well. If we all did this for just one person in our lives, how much better the world would be! Mental hospitals would be much emptier too, and not just because a lot of pathetic, sick patients had been turned out into the streets.

Six

ABSENT HEALING

Speak to Him, thou, for He hears,
And Spirit with Spirit can meet —
Closer is He than breathing,
And nearer than hands or feet.

Alfred, Lord Tennyson (1809–92)

Before we go any further, I should like to introduce you to Toby. Toby is a cat. He was found on the roadside very thin and covered in fleas, and with a bad wound in his leg and was taken in by the RSPCA. Luckily for him, he found a kind lady to give him a home.

I have a soft spot for Toby because once, when he was ill, I was able to give him absent healing with happy results. His owner was good enough to write me a letter putting the event on record. Her account runs:

One morning — it was 5 February 1989 — I came down to find him in apparent discomfort. He didn't seem to be able to walk properly and was very distressed. I took him to the vet immediately. The vet diagnosed FUS — Feline Urological Syndrome which I had never heard of! Apparently, it is caused by a build-up of crystals in the bladder which break down to a fine sandy substance which, in turn, blocks the urethra and prevents the cat from passing water.

He had an operation to clear this but after two days he was blocked again. More operations followed. The vet

89

allowed me to pick him up after ten days. He is about ten years old and the operations had exhausted him. Later the same evening it became clear that he was blocked again. I was distraught. I couldn't face taking him back to the vet and putting him through more pain. Then I remembered that my sister, who is a journalist, had interviewed a healer. Not being a great believer in that sort of thing, I had only listened with half an ear. Later that evening I rang Betty Shine. She instantly knew what Toby's problem was. I felt very guilty at this stage because I had been so cynical about her. She asked me to sit with Toby on my knee and place my hand on his bladder.

That hour was one of the strangest I have ever spent. My emotions were so mixed up with guilt and desperation. Toby was quite calm at the start. Then he began to get restless and his tail was swishing about. After an hour I phoned Betty and she told me to take him upstairs and let him sleep on my bed.

My husband Paul, already unimpressed that I had resorted to ringing a healer, was even more so by the prospect of Toby on the bed. I was adamant. Whilst I was getting undressed Toby jumped down off the bed, went to his tray and had a wee! 'Betty's done it,' I screeched.

All this happened a year ago. Toby is now bursting with health, and the vet was totally dumbfounded when I took him in for his recent check-up. He said that as he hadn't heard from me he thought Toby must have died. If it hadn't been for the healing I believe he would have done. I only have to mention Betty's name and Toby is by my side purring. There is no more cynicism in our house when healing is mentioned.

What did I do during that crucial hour when Toby was being healed? I sat down quietly, closed my eyes and projected my thoughts on to Toby and his owner, thus linking up with the network. I then performed the operation known as 'topping up' – that is I beamed my energy on to Toby's owner so that she in turn could pass it through her hands to the cat. I then drew energy back through the cat's bladder so as to break down the crystals. The ability to harness energy enables one to perform all sorts of 'operations'. This was a simple one.

Many people assume that all healing must be psychosomatic. They argue that what cures sufferers is the faith these people have in the healer, in this case myself. The story of Toby the cat shows that this belief is wide of the mark. For one thing, a cat could hardly have 'faith' in an unknown healer. For another, both the owner and her husband were initially sceptical.

If it was simple faith, why are so many people cured by healers with whom they have previously had no contact, who are complete strangers to them, rather than by their doctors with whom they probably have a good rapport? Simply having trust in another person's powers does not do the trick. If only it did!

For sixteen years I have been giving absent healing to people and animals all over the world. My first book, *Mind to Mind*, was published in January 1989 and since that time I have received hundreds of letters and telephone calls every week from people asking for appointments on a one-to-one basis. For obvious reasons, this soon became impossible. What I have been able to offer instead is absent healing. What is this healing?

All life is energy. Therefore thought, being a projection of the mind towards someone or something, is energy too. Over the years, by a projection of my own thought, I have constructed a powerful network of healing energy all over the world. When I ask someone to think of me, that person immediately makes contact with me through the mind, and this projection of the patient's mind further helps to build up the network. Imagine a grid of healing energy all over the world and perhaps you will be better able to picture what I mean. It is not necessary that patients should know they are being helped and indeed many do not. The link with me may be made by a third person — the one who has asked me to help some relation or friend.

Of course absent healing does not always bring a cure. Sometimes the physical body is so broken down with illness or riddled with disease that a permanent cure is impossible. The question is, how much rejuvenation can be given and will it have any effect? Sometimes a patient who is terminally ill appears to achieve a miraculous recovery very soon after the healing has begun, only to relapse again two or three days later. But miracles do happen and I have received countless letters confirming recovery and cure.

Finally, here is an extraordinary and very human

story which I think deserves quoting at length. The lady who wrote this account is a great friend.

My husband had left for London on business and would be away for a few days. As the car disappeared around the corner the telephone rang. It was my daughter, Jacqui. She was very distressed and managed to tell me, between sobs, that my mother, her grandmother, had been taken to hospital very ill and was on the danger list.

It appeared that my mother, who lives alone, had haemorrhaged badly from a burst vein in her leg and had just managed to dial 999 before she lost consciousness. The police traced the call and had to break into her flat to get to her. By that time she had lost a great deal of blood and was suffering from hypothermia. She was rushed to hospital and my daughter was contacted as she lived quite close by. We ourselves lived some 80 miles away in Sussex.

I was in great difficulty as I had hurt my back and could only walk with a stick. I just didn't know what to do. Betty is a dear friend, so I phoned her in total panic.

Betty said, very calmly: 'Don't worry. Hire a car to get to your mother – I'll look after the rest and give her absent healing. She *is* very ill, but she will be all right.'

The car was hired and within three hours I was by my mother's bedside. She looked absolutely awful. She was being given a blood transfusion as she had lost three pints of blood. She was wrapped in foil and looked barely alive. A nurse was with her constantly and there was doubt whether she would recover. (She was unconscious still.)

I stayed for the rest of the day and there was little improvement. At last, unable to stay any longer, I went home to her flat for some rest. The hospital would tell me if I was needed.

When I got home I phoned Betty and told her the news. 'She'll be all right,' said Betty, 'I'm working very hard on her.'

When I got to the ward the next morning I could not believe my eyes! There was mother – sitting up in bed looking almost her old self. She was still having transfusions but she could talk to me and said she was feeling well although very tired. She didn't remember much of what had happened – her last memory was of dialling 999. She did, however, say she'd dreamt she was in a most beautiful garden with flowers of unbelievable colours.

I just couldn't believe it. Yesterday I really did think she would die and today . . . The doctors and nurses were rather bewildered by the change in her and put it down to Mum being 'tough'. I told them of Betty's healing but they didn't react too much to this.

As soon as I could I phoned Betty. 'I know she is better,' she said when I told her about the remarkable recovery. 'I saw her last night.' She went on to tell me that she had 'travelled' to my mother's bedside. She told me the colours of the flowers on her locker – described the nurse perfectly and even told me the colour of the doctor's hair, how scruffy he looked, and the colour of his trousers. All totally accurate. She also described my father and my grandmother who, she said, were by the bedside. Both of them had died many years before.

In actual fact Betty had not left her home in Sussex but her mind had travelled to help my mother. Unbelievable, but wonderfully true.

It took several weeks and a lot of care by the nurses and doctors for my mother to regain her strength, but if it hadn't been for Betty's astounding and wonderful help, perhaps she wouldn't have recovered at all, or at best after a very, very, long time.

This happened three years ago. Mum is still going strong and will be eighty this year.

How do I manage to achieve such results? The key, of course, is MIND ENERGY. As soon as a person thinks about me and before he or she has even put pen to paper or lifted the telephone, the link is automatically made. Then as soon as the letter or telephone call is received, I slip the name into the network. The thought is the deed, and every day, twice a day, my thoughts go out to all those I am trying to help – and to animal patients too. This sounds like magic – and in fact it is! Not only do I make the contact but my thoughts are picked up by my spirit friends, without whose help the success rate would not be impressive. However, my patients have to make the first move and ask for help before I, as the medium, can complete the circuit.

Try thinking of me and asking me for help, at nine o'clock in the morning and again at nine o'clock at night. Just to see what happens. A letter may not even be necessary. Experiment with your own thoughts and know, without a shadow of a doubt, that you are contacting someone.

Don't be ashamed to ask for help. All of us need to do so from time to time.

Asking for help or merely tuning in, either to me

or to some other healing network, is a positive step on the road to healing yourself and other people. Try it – both ways. If you wish to heal someone living a long way away, perhaps even abroad, all you have to do is to sit quietly and think of that person, asking for help in the manner that I have explained or simply thinking of a well-known healer. Automatically this will link you into a healing network, mine or another. Part of your mind energy, that is, your life force, will be reaching the person you wish to heal even before you have finished thinking of his or her name. All things are known! Don't forget too, that, as I have said before, every act of healing will benefit yourself as well. By projecting your mind outwards you link it up with cosmic energy. Thus your energy counterpart will be opened up, your vortices (or chakras) and meridians cleared, your congestive energy and unwelcome pressures released. Everything that goes out must return in the fullness of time. Heal others, and you will heal yourself also.

In the next chapter I will tell you about another way of practising self-healing, and more generally of developing your spiritual awareness. That way is through the knowledge and use of mantras.

Seven

MANTRAS AND THE WONDERS OF SOUND

The only elevation of a human being consists in the exercise, growth, energy of the higher principles and powers of his soul. A bird may be shot upwards to the skies by a foreign force; but it rises, in the true sense of the word, only when it spreads its own wings and soars by its own living power.

Channing

The first fact to grasp if you are to understand the principle of Mantra is that sound creates vibration and vibration creates energy – psychic energy, which can be found deep within you. Through listening to mantric sound you will begin to discover a more positive side to your nature, a side that will enable you to grow and progress in a very individual way. Mantric sound awakens latent energies which can heal both the mind and the body. It has been doing this for thousands of years and in all walks of life.

But what is Mantra? (My daughter Janet has recorded tapes in which she demonstrates mantric sound and instructs you in its use. These are available from the address at the back of the book.) Most people, before they have had personal experience of it, would reply, if questioned, that they think mantric sound is 'some sort of humming'. As you will learn by listening to Janet's voice on the tape, it is rather more than that! It is in fact a very subtle sort of sound, sometimes sung in the form of one key note, sometimes as a simple tune.

Many people, when they feel tension or stress entering their lives, deal with it in a physical way by going out and taking exercise. This is fine within its limits. It tones up the body and momentarily banishes the cares. But Mantra is an altogether more penetrating technique. Listen on the tape to those very special sound vibrations. You will become aware of the change taking place within you. Do the exercises too. Now will be the time to break down any barriers you may have built around yourself and in so doing to gain a better understanding not only of yourself but of others. You will become aware of the rhythms within you. You will feel your heart beat. You will feel that time has no beginning and no end. Just listen to the sounds. You have within you your own natural flow of rhythm, and as you breathe in and out you will feel your energies becoming more and more intense.

Now you will have taken your very first steps towards understanding your innermost feelings. Your relief, as you shed all negativity, will be tremendous. Mind and spirit are free at last, and laughter, love and happiness are beginning to surround you. Try the method and see.

Mantra is derived from *man* meaning 'thought' and *tra*, which stems from the word indicating 'protection'. Therefore Mantra is a method of protecting yourself from, and taking yourself beyond, thought, which is the very thing that prevents you from experiencing the whole self. Mantra is often related to prayer but although to a certain extent the two are comparable, prayer is expressed spontaneously and always bears some sort of message, whereas Mantra *is* the message! Mantra is very often described as chanting. But this cannot cover the whole meaning of the word. Mantra is designed to stabilize all thought waves and bring harmony and complete awareness, where there is no object or subject, only a state of being.

You may be interested if I give you, by way of Janet's researches, the scientific point of view. Mantras are fundamental in determining the shape of objects in the universe, and scientists have shown that under vibrations caused by Mantra, small particles of matter group themselves together in definite geometrical patterns and figures, corresponding exactly to the quality, strength and rhythm of sound. Thus the frequency of sound energy influences the forms which emerge when that energy becomes visible.

Over two hundred years ago the German physician Ernest Chladni discovered that he could make vibration patterns visible. He mounted a thin metal plate on a violin, scattered sand on the plate, and found that when the violin was played the sand arranged itself into the most beautiful patterns. These arrangements were known as Chladni's figures and developed because the sand only comes to rest on those parts of the plate where there is no vibration. They have been used extensively in physics to demonstrate wave function and they illustrate very clearly that different frequencies produce different formal patterns. These patterns can also be seen in organic forms such as the rings on a tree trunk, the stripes of the tiger and the hexagonal grids of insect mounds, etc. One could go on indefinitely with examples, since all things are transformed in some way by vibration.

Living organisms select from the barrage of electromagnetic waves in their environment only those frequencies likely to contain the best information. For instance, bats see with their ears, building up an accurate picture of their environment by sending out high frequency sounds and listening to the patterns in the return echoes.

During the past ten years Hans Jenny, a scientist from Switzerland, has been able to use an invention called a 'tonoscope' which converts sounds into visible three-dimensional patterns in inert material. The human voice is used as the sound source, and when the letter 'O' is spoken into the microphone, it produces a perfectly spherical pattern. The sphere is one of nature's basic forms, but it is amazing to find that the shape produced by the frequency of the 'O' sound is exactly the shape to have been chosen to use in script. From this experiment I feel that we can safely say that words have a power of their own virtue stemming from their own special frequencies. This raises the question whether chants, sacred formulas or even magic words have an influence in relation to other sounds chosen at random. It appears that they do. Lyall Watson says in his book *Supernature*: 'In the beginning was the word.' But St John said: 'In the beginning was the sound of the world.' Every organism interprets the universal rhythms in its own way; space and time exist outside of individual awareness.

Now let me move on to the vibrations of Mantra in relation to our physical bodies. Within the body we have sensory receptors, sight, hearing, taste and smell. The body has the means of detecting a wide variety of sensations, arising from within and without, affecting the gross body completely. The vibrations come about by external or internal stimuli which are picked up by the sensory organs.

To give a very basic example, when Mantra is performed the stimulus is the voice and, in turn, the vibration is picked up by the ear. All messages sent to or from the brain travel through the central nervous system which lies within the vertebral column and skull (*Sushumna*). All sensory receptors can be compared to the microphone which converts mechanical input into electrical output. This can explain why when practising Mantra, the attention is drawn toward the centre of the body, very often following the vortices from the base of the spine to the top of the head. One thing is certain, the vibrations caused by Mantra are very powerful indeed, and need to be mastered under some form of guidance, preferably a regular teacher well versed in the subject.

Everything in the universe originates in, and is

constituted of, sound. It has been demonstrated that muscles under tension produce audible sound: research has shown that everything, everywhere, emits sound, even if it is too low or too high to hear.

The physical sound patterns produced by Mantras are capable of coming into sympathetic vibration with patterns made up of physical phenomena. Just as ultrasonic waves destroy bacteria, so Mantras have been used in the form of healing through these sound waves.

It is not just superstition, it is fact, and through various pitches of sound vibration, illnesses of the mind and body have been cured. That is why Mantra is an important part of this book and why I am giving you this scientific explanation. The insistent repetition of Mantra sets up a pattern of sound vibrations which can, in time, completely alter the state of consciousness.

The vibration caused through Mantra is the power that transports the mind from its normal state to superconsciousness. By the use of man's will he is able to melt the vibration of his solid physical body into cosmic energy and, in turn, can transform this energy into mental energy. The Gita refers to this power: 'He who realizes the truth of my prolific manifestations and the (creative and dissolving) power of my divine Yoga is unshakeably united (to me). This is beyond doubt.' – *Bhagavad Gita X:7*.

There is a very interesting ancient medical discipline dating from 3000 to 1000 B.C., originating back in ancient India, from which most western medicine is derived, and this therapy is called 'Ayurveda' (from *ayur* meaning 'life' and *veda* meaning 'knowledge' or 'science'). The science of life is an addition to a Hindu sacred writing dating from 1200 B.C. – the Artharva Veda. It is said that this school of medicine is responsible for the health of 80–90 per cent of people in India today.

This form of medicine is mainly concerned with the levels of the individual mind: Rajas, relating to active, creating energy; Tamas, relating to passive or destroying energy; and Satva, relating to unifying and preserving energy. Ayurveda aims at centring upon these states, but this form of medicine is not related to the physical system of medicine, as it is in the West. Rather it operates in all levels of man through ceremonies, Yogic breathing and of course, Mantras. This can be classed as one of the fringe medicines and is a total way of life to the practitioner, capturing and combining his religious beliefs and his medical practice.

Even in the therapies now practised in the West the role of Mantra is important, even if not always acknowledged. In hypnosis, for instance, the voice of the hypnotist controls the suggestibility of the patient, depending on the tone and vibration of the sounds made.

There is also a technique called sound therapy which involves the generating of sound waves by electronic devices. These waves are then delivered to the body by an applicator which is placed over the part needing treatment. The frequencies generated by the disease, being undesirable, are cancelled out, and healing is allowed to proceed. The applicator is a simple hand-held instrument which delivers sound from magnetic tapes. When a person is having sound therapy he or she may or may not hear the vibrations; this is because the frequency is adjusted so that it relates only to one particular part of the body. Each tissue in the body and every organ has its own vibrating frequency which can be altered by the application of sound waves. Sound therapists maintain that all our organs and cells behave rather like the heart, and that all disease is manifested by a change in the fundamental frequency of the vibration of energy output of the body. This change can take place in a group of cells, a whole body organ or over the entire body. Sound therapy aims at bringing the vibrations back to normal.

Another interesting aspect of sound and vibration is that related to ultrasonography. Since the early 1960s it has been used to examine foetuses for abnormalities. It can detect features ten times smaller than those shown by X-ray, and what is more, it is far cheaper to buy than X-ray equipment. Within the next few years newer ultrasound machines are expected to have reached a degree of sophistication that promises to revolutionize the field of ultrasound medicine.

There is the possibility of producing ultrasound 'signatures' of healthy or diseased tissues, enabling doctors to identify malignant or benign tumours without recourse to painful biopsies. The principle behind ultrasound is amazingly simple. Sound frequencies up to five million cycles per second – well beyond the range that can be heard by the most sensitive animal ears – are bounced off a foetus (or body organ) to create echoes. Ultrasonography is a spin-off of sonar.

One last example of how vibration is revolutionizing our system is the work of Dr Reginald C. Eggleton of the Indiana University Medical School. He is studying the effect of drugs on individual heart cells as well as tracing the pathway of nerve impulses that travel out from the heart when it is stimulated by a pacemaker. These cells no longer have to be stained to be seen but can now be viewed in their natural state by an acoustic microscope.

Through Mantra the inner sound, the *nada*, is awakened. This is the most subtle aspect of this wonderful method of soothing, liberating and healing. Mantra leads to a dissolving of the image and concept and this is called *laya*. 'Lord Siva has shown innumerable paths to *laya*, but it seems to me that the practice of *nada* is the best of them all.' When practising Mantra the initial attention is drawn toward the vibrations caused in time through the experience of the person so engaged, these vibrations then slowly change into an inner light which shines out from the body (*aura*).

Mantra helps to illuminate the Ego by directing all attention, though in a relaxed and peaceful way, towards union with the universe, transcending all thought and just being, uniting with the one energy that governs all things. We know that the solid human body can be reduced to liquids and evaporated into invisible gases, but man has not yet learned the link between mind and body, spirit and matter. He has not yet learned how to bring it back to its original form. It is said that vibrating energy becomes, at the highest level, pure consciousness but that, vibrating at increasingly gross rates, it manifests as the body. This is one interpretation of the word Mantra ('protection from thought') – a divine communion attained through devotional, concentrated repetition of root-word sounds that have a spiritually beneficial vibratory potency. I love this particular definition.

Mantra or Sound Vibration is the vibration of all that is. It is said to be God. It is the principle of being. In St John's Gospel the Evangelist starts by saying: 'In the beginning was the Word, and the word was with God, and the word was God.' The word for the Tibetans is *Hum*, for the Moslems *Amin*, for the Egyptians, Greeks, Romans, Jews and Christians *Amen*. You cannot have the idea of God without the word, as the idea and the word are inseparable.

Many people are frightened (because this is what they have been told) that Mantra is harmful, that it can bring on fits, hallucinations, and so on. But like anything else, if it is performed with the right attitude of mind it can only have the correct effect. Let us be honest and say that the mind will govern how the energy produced will travel, whether it be for good or ill! You could repeat the word 'Apple' and if you really believed it was harmful, it would produce a bad effect. So being able to explain the truly positive qualities of Mantra is the very first step, making it clear that Mantra has a very strong healing quality, and that the vibrations caused can be directed to those various parts of the mind or body in need.

My daughter's methods when teaching a class are a good lesson in how this should be done. First, she likes the class to form a circle, thus transferring the vibration from one person to another and allowing the energies to flow through in a never-ending journey. Then she has them sitting in a comfortable position so that the total consciousness is taken away from the body; this is most important. If you are uncomfortable the practice of Mantra, especially in its meditational forms, will not work. The class are asked to use a simple rhythmic breath. This helps to prepare the mind and body, gently massaging the lungs and allowing them to expand, eventually enabling them to take in the full capacity of breath which is used during Mantra.

So now the class is ready. Their minds are calmed, their lungs massaged, their heart beats slowed and the breath regulated. Now it is explained to them that when the Mantra is repeated, it can be used to gain control of the mind, bringing it into a state of one-pointedness, for the healing of mind and body. Its use will expand the vortices, speed up the vibrationary rate, and cleanse the aura. For whichever process the individual student wishes to use Mantra, he or she can direct the vibrations and sounds accordingly.

There are many different Mantras that can be used, such as the Bija Mantras from the Sanskrit alphabet which relate to the vortex, or chakra, system. Each vortex centre has a vibrationary relationship with sound, the first centre resonating to middle C, the second to D, and so on until we reach the seventh vortex. So there are seven sounds, seven colours and seven centres which can be related to when practising Bija Mantra. And there are many other Mantras, even a Mantric alphabet!

Now comes the moment when the session must be brought to an end. My daughter encourages her class to quieten very gradually the sound being produced; this is far better than just stopping dead. So the vibrations and sound come to a gentle ebb and flow, and when the sound eventually disappears the consciousness goes out into the universe to be used for universal matters leaving the gross physical body behind. The consciousness is guided back and the class slowly starts to breathe naturally, becoming aware once again of the heart beat. But this process should be taken very slowly indeed if you want to achieve the maximum effect. It is not suited to beginners, who would find it very difficult without some kind of guidance.

I have asked Janet for her thoughts on this chapter and here they are:

'We are all individual. We all need something that we can use to promote the health of the mind, the body and the spirit. And as you grow up and progress in your life you gradually find out the different methods that are best suited to you, because you are individual, you are very special and you must be able to use something that you feel comfortable with. I've been learning about Mantra for quite a few years now and I have found that for me it is the most suitable way of expanding my mind and healing myself. Also, when you practise Mantra and laying the hands on other people and healing them, those vibrations go through into those patients and help them.

'Mantra is a very special art and should be learned very slowly and gradually. You don't even have to be able to sing in tune. In fact, in a class where you have people singing out of tune it produces a quite wonderful effect. After the practice of Mantra you can feel very tearful, and this is because you have let go of those nasty negative energies and you feel free. You can also feel very high, just as though you could fly through the air like a bird. But whatever experience you have it will be totally different to those of your neighbours. In every single way we are all different. The voice is like a fingerprint; no two people have the same set. So remember, Mantra is just one other way of expanding yourself.

'There are many different kinds of Mantra that can be used. There is either one key note, or root note, or a very simple tune, as this chapter has already explained. But it is the constant repetition of that tune or note that creates the intensity of vibration. When actually practising your self-Mantra, you use the tongue, the back of the throat, the whole of the mouth, and you manipulate the voice in such a way that the sound vibration is taken right up into the sinuses and into the top of the head. This is where the psychic energy is stored. By vibrating the vortex situated in the forehead and the top of the head you awaken those latent psychic energies which help, especially, to heal the mind. You are having to pin-point your awareness on to that one sound to the exclusion of all thought.

'In everything we do, whether it is learning a language or playing an instrument, we have need of a firm foundation. Now, when developing the vortices, for instance, you must first know what each vortex represents, so look back to chapter Two to refresh your memory on this.

'Finally, let me repeat, there will never be two plants or two people or two sounds exactly alike. Each sound will be completely different every single time. That's what makes Mantra unique. It is ever changing, just as we as individuals change every second and every minute and every hour and every day, and should be allowed to change, all the time. In that way we progress in our spirits and in our minds, so that eventually we understand the different dimensions that are around us.'

If you have followed the explanations so far in this

book and practised the exercises a sufficient number of times to feel that you are becoming at least reasonably proficient in them, you will find that your life has already begun to change. But, you may tell me, all this has been quite hard work! I agree, and I have never pretended that these wonderful improvements can happen effortlessly or overnight.

The next section of this book will move on from methods of healing to some common-sense advice on how we should live our daily lives – what attitudes we should have, even what we should eat and drink. For we are body as well as spirit and unless we are sensible in down-to-earth ways, the wonderful 'mind magic' which is the subject of this book is likely to remain sadly grounded!

Before we move on, however, the next chapter offers some light relief – strange happenings which you may find you can parallel in the experiences of yourself or your friends; a selection of exercises that are meant to be fun but can also be put to immediate practical use; a group of assorted skills through which you can increase your psychic awareness; and finally, a series of questions and answers based on the information given in this book and indeed on all my teachings and my experience as a healer and medium. The questions listed are taken from among those which patients and readers have been putting to me over the years. Therefore I know you will find them interesting and useful.

So cheer up – not all work needs to be painful!

Eight

FOUR AFTERTHOUGHTS

This is not the end. It is not even the beginning of the
end. But it is, perhaps, the end of the beginning.

Winston Churchill in his Mansion House speech on
10 November 1942, referring to the Desert War.

AFTERTHOUGHT ONE:
STRANGE HAPPENINGS

The Table Top

While taking a rest at a hotel on the South Coast and
enjoying a peaceful breakfast in my room, I heard a
voice telling me to go to a nearby town, of which I
was given the name. There I would find something
to go over the fireplace in my new house. I sat
rooted to the spot, because the last conversation
I'd had with Alan was about the new fireplace he
had been building and how it would be nice to have
something large, in copper, hanging above it. We had
both decided that, whatever it was, it would be too
expensive!

Before I finished my breakfast I telephoned the
receptionist and asked her where this particular town
was. She said it was about ten minutes away by taxi.

I dressed, called a taxi, and set off on my journey.
The taxi driver asked me where I would like to be

dropped. I thought if those above had given me the message they would know, so I replied, 'Wherever you think.' The taxi stopped. I looked across the road. We had pulled up outside a covered antique market.

Upon entering the market I went straight through the building to the back and there, in front of me, was a huge table top in copper! I looked at the price and could not believe my eyes. It was £47 and worth about four times that amount.

I bought it and went outside, looking for a taxi to take me back to the hotel. Across the road was a bookshop. Being a book addict, I decided there was no way I was going back to the hotel without taking a peep inside. As I walked in, right in front of my eyes was a large hardback book by Sai Baba, the amazing Indian sage whose work I have already described. I couldn't believe it: not every bookshop has Sai Baba's books. I asked the owner why he stocked them. He said: 'I don't usually, but someone suggested I should order one copy to see if it sold, and there it is.' I bought it, as it was only recently published and I hadn't seen it before. The owner laughed: 'Perhaps I'll order a few more since this one's gone so quickly.'

When I got back to the hotel I took a more leisurely look at my newly acquired table top. It was about 28 inches in diameter, and I saw that it was engraved with a map of Marco Polo's Silk Route to China. It has pride of place on the wall above our fireplace, a very special item.

Have you ever experienced a coincidence of this sort? If so, why not write to me, at the address at the back of this book, and tell me about it? Meanwhile, ponder the following even stranger pair of occurrences.

Daffodils

In my first book I mentioned the medium who forecast that Alan, my present companion, would come to live with me when the daffodils were out, which he did. A year after my book was published, and a day before the anniversary of Alan's arrival, he opened the back door to let the dogs out for the last time that night. There, lying on the step, were eight miniature jonquils lovely to look at and with a most exquisite scent. We had nothing like that growing in the garden, and certainly nobody could have got round the back of the house to leave them there – there was absolutely no means of access. Neither of us could understand their sudden materialization.

We had a friend staying the night who rose before we did to let the dogs out into the garden in the morning. Imagine his amazement when on the back doorstep he saw a dozen huge daffodils wet with the morning dew. He brought them in and we all sat staring at them in disbelief. Again, there was no possible way of explaining how they had got there.

Phenomena like these are always unexpected and always tell you something. What they are telling you is: 'Someone is always around – to encourage you and give you that necessary helping hand.'

Now here is something that happened to Alan himself. It reads like a fictional ghost story, only it happens to be true. The following is his own account.

Alan's Story

In the early 60s I worked in offices on the first floor of a listed building just off Russell Square, close to the British Museum. The basement of the building was, in fact, used to house a library of records belonging to the museum. The floor above had been gutted during the blitz and was sealed off awaiting renovation.

The winter was severe, and the forecast one morning was for heavy snow throughout the day. Since I lived about 30 miles from the office, I decided to take my sleeping bag in case I couldn't get home. In fact, the forecast proved correct, and it snowed all day in Central London bringing all forms of transport to a virtual standstill. As I had no alternative but to spend the night in the office I decided to make the most of it and, donning my overcoat and wellington boots, another wise precaution following the morning forecast, I made my way to St Martin's Lane and was successful in getting a ticket for that popular satirical success, *Beyond the Fringe*.

When I left the theatre it was still snowing heavily so, after a bite to eat at a café, I made my way back to the office. The street door was fastened by a Yale lock which I secured on the inside so that not even a key holder could enter. The door on the landing of the first floor which gave access to our suite of offices was also secured with a Yale lock.

Having arranged some easy chairs from the reception area as a bed, I closed the door of my office, undressed, and climbed into my sleeping bag. I am not a nervous type and do not suffer from an over-active imagination. I felt no apprehension, although there was that peculiar hush which results from the deadening effect of heavy snow. It was one of those rare occasions when London was as silent as the countryside.

I have never had any trouble falling asleep and that evening was no exception.

I awoke with a shock in the early hours of the morning. There was a loud knocking, apparently on the landing door leading into the offices. I lay rigid in my sleeping bag. Suddenly the stillness and the pale reflection of the snow through the window took on a new significance. I convinced myself I must have been dreaming and was just settling down to sleep when the knocking started again. It was by my right ear, as I had positioned the bed across the door.

I climbed out of my sleeping bag and hastily put on my trousers, jacket and shoes. Having switched on the light in the entrance hall I undid the Yale lock and opened the door. There was no-one there. I walked up the next flight of stairs to the gutted top floor. It was securely bolted. I then went downstairs to the front door and opened it and peered into the street. There was not a soul in sight, just a white, silent carpet of snow. And there were no footprints!

It was bitterly cold and I hurried back to my office locking all the doors behind me.

I lay on my bed trying to find a logical explanation for the knocking. There seemed to be no answer. I was about to undress for the second time that night when the knocking started again. Though I was convinced I wouldn't find anyone, I opened the landing door once more. There was no-one there. I decided to get into bed, as by this time I was cold and tired.

The next morning I went down to the basement to see the curator of the library and told him of my experience. He said that although he hadn't heard of any previous happenings he did know that a couple had died instantly when the building was bombed.

I was very keen to spend another night in the office with other witnesses but we moved out to better premises soon afterwards and the opportunity did not recur.

Alan maintains that this experience pales beside the incredible phenomena he has witnessed since living with me, but every psychic experience is thrilling to the one who witnesses it.

As readers of my last book will be aware, my granddaughter Raina, Janet's daughter, is extremely psychic, like her mother and myself. We very rarely speak about our work in front of her but now she is growing up she is aware of what we do. She, too, has had many psychic experiences, of which the following is an example.

One day when she had been playing in her bedroom, she ran downstairs to ask her mother why a certain man, who was obviously a spirit visitor, had visited her three times. 'I don't know,' Janet replied. 'Did you ask the man his name?'

Raina replied: 'Yes, he said his name was Herbert.' This is a rather old-fashioned name for a child to come out with nowadays, but Alan's father's name was Herbert. He loved children and was always appearing to us when we occupied the house before we sold it to Janet. But everyone knew him as Bertie. Only Alan knew his full name!

I could recount hundreds of psychic experiences from the letters I receive after giving absent healing. There is no doubt that when the energies are raised by exercises or healing one is able to see into other dimensions. If you have had a psychic experience that cannot be explained logically, please write it down and send it to the address at the back of this book. I believe that people are far more open about their experiences than they used to be, so do let me know of yours.

Here, to encourage you, are some accounts by people who have received absent healing from me with a bonus!

'While I was receiving healing from you at nine o'clock at night I saw my father for the first time since he died. He was standing in the room smiling at me. The vision lasted for about a minute, and I have felt better ever since.'

'I was lying in bed thinking of you when suddenly at the foot of my bed I saw my ginger cat who died four years ago. I was absolutely amazed and still can't get over it. He looked so contented. Now I know there is no need to grieve any more. He is still very much alive!'

'I woke one morning with a fright and there standing beside my bed was my grandmother. She smiled and then disappeared.'

'While tuning into you at nine o'clock this morning I saw someone in a white robe. The vision only lasted for a split second, but I was so surprised because I am not in the least "religious".'

'While I was meditating and thinking of your name I saw a blue swirl of energy. It sped all round the room and vanished. Since then I have felt absolutely fantastic.'

'Do all your patients see a white light when they think of you? Every time I think of you this bright white light enters the room and it is so peaceful. I feel so much better now.'

So many people have written to me about such phenomena that I could go on quoting endlessly. But these examples will I hope be enough to convince you that you too can have experiences of this sort once your energy levels are raised.

But now, on to the exercises.

AFTERTHOUGHT TWO: EXERCISES TO GIVE YOU ZIP!

Stay the Pangs!

I had an interesting conversation with a friend of mine the other day. He was telling me about his great-uncle who was a painter, and who used to suffer from tremendous pangs of hunger from time to time.

When this happened he used to paint a plate of food and then slowly rub it out. When he had finished he felt as though he had actually eaten the food. I was extremely interested in this story as it sums up what I am trying to teach. What my friend's uncle had done was to make energy food – and like everything else you make with energy, this became a reality.

If you are feeling hungry when you happen to be reading this book, try the method for yourself. Sit down, close your eyes, and imagine you are eating the most delicious foods you can think of. Taste the different flavours, savour them, see yourself enjoying them and feel your stomach filling up. If you can't visualize them just know that you are eating them. Believe me, it works. This exercise is also an ideal one for slimmers. You can have all the chocolate bars you want and never put on weight!

Mirror Image

Sit down in a chair in a quiet room and close your eyes. A spirit helper is going to put his hands on your head and as he does so you will sense a tingling all over your body. You will then begin to feel completely relaxed. Your eyes will be closed and you will feel a heaviness in your feet slowly creeping up you until your body is 'paralysed' and you are unable to move.

You are now in a state of complete relaxation, and whatever you have wrong with you will begin to disappear. If you haven't anything wrong with you, you will still feel energy surging through your body as it is rejuvenated. If you are elderly, you will begin to feel as though you have shed many years. You will feel the circulation renewed, the blood flowing through your whole body, cleansing it, removing toxins. Your skin will feel clearer, your eyes brighter, your wrinkles will be removed. Any excess skin around the neck will tighten up, and your whole body will be tingling with the incredible feeling of health and youth.

Whatever age you are, you are now giving yourself your first Beauty Treatment of the Mind – the most wonderful beauty treatment of your life. You on your own. You are your own surgeon. Whatever you want to happen to your body will happen. You no longer feel lost and powerless to do things for yourself.

Now someone has brought you a full-length mirror. Look into it. You will see for yourself what an incredible change has taken place. You will enjoy looking at yourself, knowing that with regular treatment the new you will emerge. Eventually you will not have to look into your imaginary mirror all the time, only when you feel the need to do so.

Take at least ten minutes to carry out this exercise. It will change your life and your looks. Believe me, it really works, for whilst you have been imagining all these changes you have been giving instructions to your body and training it to carry out the instructions of your mind. By so doing you have reversed the age process and the message will be picked up loud and clear by your body's cells. All cells have a 'mind of

121

their own', responsive to your own mind, and will appreciate a full set of instructions.

Instant Recall

This exercise is to enable you to file away information so that you can recall it at any time.

Once again I would like you to sit quietly and breathe deeply three times. Once you have done this I want you to see or know that there is a row of filing cabinets in your room. On top of the filing cabinets you will find labels and a pen. I want you to write these labels as follows: 1. Universal Mind, 2. Environment, 3. Healthy Food, 4. Vitamins and Minerals, 5. Ability to Heal, 6. Miscellaneous. These are only a few suggestions; you can write any number of labels with the titles of your choice.

Now try to remember something you have read in this book that you have found interesting and would like to remember. Make out another label to fit it (unless of course, it suits one of the above). Choose your file, open the drawer, take out a folder and file the information away. When you have replaced the folder in the file, look at the label on the front again, and remember which file it is in. Then push the drawer closed. Now you will have instant recall when you want to remember that particular piece of information. The method is simply to think of your file. Think of the label on the outside, open the file, take out the appropriate folder, and look inside. As you become more proficient all you will have to do is think of the Universal Mind and everything will be revealed!

Carry on in this way, filing away all sorts of information. It can be very interesting, especially when your mind begins to feed you with information you thought you had forgotten. This will happen more and more in response to the initial stimulus, as the process gains momentum. You will probably become an addict!

Blackboard of the Mind

You must now be quite used to being told by me to sit down quietly! Don't worry. The discipline will take you into the wonderful, magical world of the imagination where everything is formed by mind energy. As I have said before many times, and will say again: energy is for ever. It can NEVER be destroyed. You are carving out your own future and the harder you work at it the greater your future will be.

So now, sit down, and when you have relaxed, close your eyes. In front of you, you will see a huge blackboard. On a ledge in front of the blackboard there will be a large piece of white chalk. Pick up the chalk and write on the blackboard everything you hate about yourself and your life. If you can't see yourself writing, just know the words are there. Keep writing. Don't give up until you have remembered everything. If you haven't enough room on the blackboard then turn it over. If you fill that side as well, then ask for another and someone will bring you one. Keep at it. When you are heartily sick of writing down all the miserable things you can remember put down the chalk.

At the side of the chair you will find a table, and on the table a damp sponge. Take the sponge and slowly wipe everything off the blackboard or blackboards. Having done that you will start feeling a whole lot better. You will have wiped the slate clean, as they say. If you do this exercise at least twice a week you will be surprised at how positive you will become, determined that never again will you allow anyone to put you down or make you feel inadequate. Remember you can always put people on your blackboard and have the pleasure of wiping them out!

Clutter

A cluttered mind is the greatest drawback anyone can have. It leaves no room for new ideas. The rubbish that has accumulated over the years is rolling around creating havoc. This exercise clears the rubbish out of your mind and leaves room for shiny, bright ideas so that your life can take on new meaning.

Sit quietly (once again!). Close your eyes and visualize a room full of tin cans, empty cardboard cartons, old bottles, masses of dirty waste paper. Add a few things for yourself until you have no room to sit down. Now take a broom and start sweeping up. In the corner of the room you will find a pile of dustbin bags. Start filling them up and put them outside for the dustman. Don't moan! If you really want a new life you have to get rid of ALL the rubbish and it isn't easy.

When you have got rid of everything – and I mean

everything – start sweeping up all the dust. Now go into the kitchen and you will find a bucket of hot water and a mop. Start washing the floor. Don't stop until your room is sparkling clean. Now relax and look around. Where before it was disgusting, you now have something to be proud of.

This is *your* mind. You have room for all the beautiful things now, don't let it get cluttered up again. It's such hard work putting it to rights.

AFTERTHOUGHT THREE: INCREASING YOUR AWARENESS

If you would like to strengthen your awareness in different ways, here are some suggestions.

Psychometry

Psychometry is a method by which you pick up impressions from a physical object.

How this works is that where you own or handle any object your energy is impressed upon it gradually in the course of time. Years later – perhaps hundreds of years later – a complete stranger can pick up that object and receive from it pictures and impressions which relate to the original owner and his or her way of life. If there have been several owners, the impressions may be hard to separate, but something is usually possible, and for that reason many mediums and clairvoyants ask to be handed some keepsake of the deceased's – a watch, ring, necklace or other item – before they give evidence, in order to help them link up.

I have myself received vivid pictures of ancient Egypt, the Pyramids, Peru and other places, with the people of those times active and in place, and many other visions of the past; and, though I have long since left that method behind, it remains, nonetheless, an excellent way of enhancing your awareness, because the accuracy of the impressions can in many cases be checked.

So try it – and first of all, experiment with a friend. A watch is the easiest article to ask for. Sit down and close your eyes and feel peaceful (you should be quite good at this by now!). Holding the object in your hand give your friend the first impression you receive from it. You may have a feeling of heat or cold – whatever you receive, pass it on. Heat usually means that the owner of the item needs healing in some way, even if only for a simple headache. Cold is quite different. It may mean that the life of the owner of the object lacks energy or is empty or that the person is simply cold. A pleasant feeling is one of gentle warmth – one usually receives the best impressions from this feeling. Now, are pictures forming in your mind? They could be of animals, people, houses, gardens, different countries. Whatever they are, continue to describe them while your friend writes them down.

Ask your friend not to interrupt or to contradict anything until after you have finished, because such doubts, if they intrude, could put you off at your first attempt. When later you are dissecting the impressions you have given, don't worry if your friend cannot make the expected link. He or she may be living with a more dominant personality, in which case it could be that person's energy which has impressed itself on the watch. If the watch had belonged to someone else for a time, it could be a mixture of energies. It is quite exciting to find out whether the impressions you received actually belonged to someone else. If it is established that they did, then this is a proof that telepathy was not involved.

On no account give impressions that you have not genuinely received. In all psychic work being true to yourself is the first principle. If you are not, you will be found out, and your reputation will end up in shreds. And if the impressions you received would be hurtful to your sitter, don't give them. As an amateur you are not there to make trouble or cause dismay.

One day I was asked to give psychometry from the wristwatch of a well-known personality. I held the watch for some time but received no impressions at all. I told this to the sitter, but when he pressed me to continue I suddenly saw a picture of a white-haired man, a little bent but with a beautiful smile. I started to relay these impressions to my sitter. 'This man is telling me that he owned the watch, that he is your grandfather, that the watch had been passed to your father who is now with him and it was passed on to you.' My sitter sat beaming. 'You are absolutely correct,' he said. I continued: 'He is showing me a red setter and black cat.' The sitter replied: 'My father had a red setter and my grandfather a black cat.' I said: 'Well, they are both with their owners.' I then continued with impressions to do with his own life.

You may say, 'That's easy for you, after all you are a medium.' How true – if this had happened during my mediumship years. Instead, it happened during the period when I was a singer and the sitter was a performer with whom I was appearing. It was a long time ago. This sort of thing could just as well happen to you. I have told the story to give you an idea of how psychic you could become in the future. It is a really exciting method.

Hand Analysis

It was through studying hand analysis for sixteen years that I developed my own mediumship and the ability to diagnose. This skill has been tested over many hundreds of years and is an excellent way to judge a person's character. Believe me, it is all in the hand!

The lines on the hand change all the time. When we are asleep we are clenching and unclenching our hands and the sub-conscious mind dictates the pressure. That is why you can see from their hands whether people worry a lot, whether they need to have spectacles, to consult a doctor and so on. There are so many diagnoses that can be made, it goes on forever. Hand analysis is not meant to be used for fortune telling. It is a science, and an extremely valuable one.

When you are proficient your own hand print will show you where your body has a disease and what vitamins and minerals you need to take to correct an imbalance. It is a mine of information.

There are many points to master. You must learn to observe and draw conclusions from the mount, the types, the consistency, flexibility, and colour of the hands, the nails, the hand as a whole, the fingers, finger tips, knotty fingers, smooth fingers, long fingers, short fingers, and the thumbs. You will learn about the line of the heart, the head, the line of life, lines of influence and of affection, the line of Saturn, of Apollo, of Mercury, the Girdle of Venus, and an infinite variety of minor lines.

Once you begin the study of the hand you will become hooked, as I was. Hands have fascinated me for years and it is the first thing I observe when I am introduced to a new acquaintance. I also scrutinize people while watching television. No matter what is being said, there are certain characteristics in the shape of the hand that often belie the speaker's words.

It is through the serious study of hand analysis that I started to make diagnoses and recommend vitamins and minerals. Many of my friends' ailments were cured in this way. It was a hobby. I have never charged a fee in all the years I practised because I was so busy doing other things. And it was always a joy. Much of the pleasure goes out of a study when one becomes professional and has to earn one's living at it but there are many very skilled hand analysts doing just that and bringing tremendous help to their clients in the process. So you too could find yourself acquiring another profession, by using your awareness in a very practical way.

I think you will find the following story amusing.

A friend of mine had a husband who was always critical of her. It seemed that in his eyes she could do nothing right, even her looks displeased him, so much so that she used to despair. One day I spent a lot of time studying her hands. I could find no reason for the criticisms at all. She had a fairly straightforward, capable, down-to-earth hand. The character analysis was very good, as I might have expected, knowing her so well. It was all rather strange. I asked her if she could persuade her husband to have his hands analysed. She said she thought there would be no chance at all, but she'd try. A week later the two of them came along together.

My first look at the husband's hands gave me an inkling of the truth but I continued my examination, giving him a character assessment as I went along. My friend was sitting with her mouth open while her husband looked distinctly put out. When I had finished she turned on him and said: 'Everything you have criticized me for belongs to you.' He looked a bit sheepish and didn't say a word.

I don't know what happened when they arrived home but my friend was never worried about her failures again. In fact she became very confident about her talents and future and made more of a success of her life than her husband did of his.

I have seen this pattern repeating itself time and again. My friend's husband was actually seeing a mirror image of himself and, although unaware of it, was blaming his wife for his own shortcomings.

If you are in this predicament, take up hand analysis. You will soon find out the truth. It is a very accurate science and something which everyone, psychic or non-psychic, can study. What it will also do is expand your awareness even more and your intuition will be second to none.

Graphology

Graphology is easy to study because a sample of handwriting takes only a minute to produce. It is invaluable whether you are an employer or an employee. Studying the handwriting of the person you might be working with could save you a lot of problems later.

I studied graphology many years ago and am always drawn back to it if I have any doubts about a person. Using this skill in conjunction with hand analysis is almost foolproof. I get the best results if I haven't met the person at all, because then my mind is clear to form an honest opinion.

Handwriting exists in such overwhelming varieties that no student of the art can ever become complacent. Every time you think you have mastered the lot, along will come someone with an entirely new sample that will keep you guessing half the night. When you are finally proved correct it is of course extremely satisfying. Businessmen making deals in which a lot of money is involved can call on graphology with great benefit. So can those who are about to get married and spend the rest of their lives together.

When you have studied this subject for a few months you will realize that there is more to it than meets the eye, but if you have stayed that long I guarantee you won't want to give up.

At one time I worked for a big organization and I used to advise them about their future employees. Of course, they didn't rely on my analysis alone but they did find it most helpful, especially if there was a choice of individuals involved.

I remember one occasion on which the firm ignored my analysis. The letter in question was from a prospective employee for a post which required that the successful applicant should be absolutely honest. From my reading I could see that the person about to be interviewed was dishonest and there were other traits I didn't like. I gave the managing director my reading and forgot about the matter. Later I found that the firm had employed this man. To say the least, I was horrified, but it was nothing to do with me and maybe anyway I was wrong. Two years passed with no trouble at all – on the surface. Then it was found that a great deal of money had been filched and cleverly covered up.

On another occasion a friend brought her prospective fiancé to dinner. He seemed to be nice and friendly with an open personality. Later, I asked for a sample of his handwriting. I only had to look at one sentence to realize that my friend was courting a criminal type. I must confess I was shocked and stayed up quite late that night to finish the analysis.

The next day my friend rang up to ask me what I had thought of her young man. I said I thought he looked very nice. She said, 'Come on, Betty. I know he looks nice. But what do you *really* think of him?' I had to tell her that the analysis of his handwriting was a bit unsavoury. There was a long silence. 'Betty,' she finally said, 'I know you are right. He has been in prison but has promised it won't happen again.' Two months later the man was back in prison and my friend finished the relationship.

Graphology is an accepted means of character analysis and is invaluable in expanding your awareness. It takes the pressure off the brain and body because you are thinking outwards and not inwards and are absorbed with something other than yourself. It is also extremely rewarding.

Numerology

Numerology means analysis through numbers. I must confess I personally have not studied numerology much, but a friend of mine, now dead, was a master of it. He used to send us readings of the names of houses, Christian names, surnames, names of streets, houses, towns – the list goes on and on. Every reading we received was accurate even though it might have taken some time to verify.

Numerology is also used as a method of character analysis using the numbers relating to the subject's names and birthdate. Like everything else it requires dedication and a lot of awareness, but if you find the idea of it attractive, so much the better.

In this chapter I have given you choices, all of which are equally fascinating and when the skills are proficiently performed, reliable. I am whetting your appetite so as to bring the wonderful world of Magic even closer. If you are interested, turn to the bibliography. The books listed there will give you enough tuition to keep you busy for years!

AFTERTHOUGHT FOUR:
QUESTIONS AND ANSWERS

Mind Expansion

Q *I have been doing the exercises at the back of your last book and although I feel healthy and more positive I haven't actually felt any different around the head. How do we know when our mind energy begins to expand?*

A You have answered your own question. The change is subtle, as all natural changes should be. What you feel or do not feel around the head is irrelevant. What is important is that you are now feeling 'healthy and more positive'. The fact that your life has improved says it all.

Q *Before I carried out the exercises on your tapes I was so negative I couldn't say boo to a goose. Now my life has changed so much that my friends say they don't recognize me and some of them add that they preferred me as I was. However, I am so successful now I don't really care what they think. Should I? I don't want to be an uncaring person.*

A   The only thing that really matters is that you are happy with *yourself* and that you are successful, whereas before you were negative and unsuccessful. The people who don't like the change will mostly be those who just want to use you. But *you* can now give others happiness because *you* are happy. If we are not happy within ourselves, how can we pass on a feeling of happiness to friends and family? Make a conscious effort to do so, and don't get upset by unjustified criticism. Don't forget – you are a walking advertisement for my methods!

Q   My husband says I have become stroppy since I have become more positive. I must say I don't really care as I have more say in our everyday life and I am certainly a lot happier. Is there anything I should guard against here?

A   I don't think being stroppy some of the time hurts a relationship at all, especially if you think there is something that needs sorting out. If you find fault and are bad-tempered, then you should start worrying. Couples should make mutual decisions – that is the only way to be content and have a successful relationship. But perhaps your husband doesn't like this idea! One of the biggest threats to living together is non-communication.

Q   When I am doing your mind-expansion exercises I sometimes have a feeling of light-headedness. Is this normal?

A   This sensation is quite common, though not everyone experiences it. It depends on how much pressure you had on your brain in the first place, when negativity was causing your mind energy to be funnelled in. The more intense it was, the more light-headed you are likely to feel as it is taken off. So don't worry. You are obviously succeeding.

Q   Is there any danger that one can expand the mind energy too much? Is there any danger that I couldn't get it back?

A   No danger at all. Even with people who practise astral travel, where the mind energy leaves the body and projects itself elsewhere, there is always a large part that never leaves. Only when your mind decides that your body has no chance of recovery will it eject itself completely.

Q   Why does the mind energy leave the bodies of perfectly healthy people who are injured in accidents but are then successfully brought back to life?

A   Shock is the cause. If there is even a remote chance that the body will recover, the mind energy will soon slip back in again.

Q   Visiting a new place, or entering a new room, I

have sometimes had the curious sensation that 'I have been here before.' Friends of mine have also experienced this from time to time. What is the explanation?

A You *have* been there before – but only a few seconds before! Your mind energy has got there before you.

Q *In MIND TO MIND you talk a lot about the different dimensions, and about moving from one dimension to another when we die. Can you explain a little more about this?*

A There is no such thing as space. There is no dividing line between one dimension and another. Dimensions are fluid energy reminiscent of oceans with their high and low tides. At high tide the linking up becomes easier, therefore the powers of psychics seem to be increased. This ebb and flow is also influenced by the planetary system.

Q *We often hear about people who talk to their plants. Is this a leg-pull?*

A No! When I was a child I used to see sparks dancing all round our house plants. These, of course, were the plants' life force. As your mind expands you will be surprised at the varied experiences your new sight will bring you. It is very exciting when these experiences suddenly occur without any warning. Then you will know that the time you have spent on

137

mind expansion exercises has not been wasted! You cannot make these experiences happen. They happen when they will.

Incidentally, there have been many experiments conducted on plants that have been fitted with electrodes and linked up to a monitor. These experiments have shown that when one plant is badly damaged, all the others go into shock, and if the person who damaged the plant re-enters the room they shrink back, but if someone who had nothing to do with causing the damage enters there is no reaction. The plants can actually identify the culprit. So you see, plants do have their own emotions and their own form of 'mind energy'. That is all the more reason for communicating with them and loving them. Who knows, perhaps as you do so you will begin to love yourself!

Energy Counterpart

Q   *In your book* MIND TO MIND *you described the chakras or vortices as whirlpools of energy that draw in life force. How do you know that it is so-called life force that is being drawn in and not some other energy that hasn't as yet been identified?*

A   It doesn't really matter what type of energy it is. The fact is that when a person's vortices stop drawing in the energy and slow down, his or her health is put at risk. That is why I call this energy life force.

Q   *What does a slowed-down vortex look like?*

A   A tangled ball of wool.

Q   *How do you untangle it?*

A   Because I can see vortices I am able to untangle them by pulling at the threads of energy that are causing the snarl-up. This gets them spinning again.

Q   *Do they have different colours?*

A   Yes, but each medium will see them differently! The colours are determined by the perception of the medium who then draws up his or her own chart for diagnosis. But the benefits will be the same if the medium is competent.

Q   *Doesn't this make it difficult for a healer to teach others?*

A   No, because not everyone has clairvoyant sight of the vortices. It is much better to teach by touch. A blocked vortex will have little or no vibration. The pupil's task is to become sensitive to what is there.

Q   *Does the same apply to meridian lines?*

A   Yes. With practice you can certainly determine where blockages have occurred.

Q   *Would you pull out the negative energy from meridian lines in the same way as from vortices?*

A   Yes. In exactly the same way.

Q   If we launch ourselves into the imaginary world of your mind exercises, could there be a danger of shutting out reality altogether?

A   None at all! The exercises are for disciplining the mind so that it becomes stronger, not weaker. Only weak minds lose their grip on reality.

Q   On conquering any bad habit it is hard not to acquire new ones. How can we avoid this?

A   By disciplining the mind.

Q   How can I achieve freedom of thought?

A   By refusing to join the rat race and declining to become yet another name on the computer. Individuality is worth any amount of effort. Try the exercises in this book.

Q   If I become more spiritual does this mean that I will have leanings towards religion?

A   Spirituality has nothing to do with religion. It means that you are 'of' spirit, at one with the universe and cosmic energy. Spirit is essence, energy. Spirituality is what you do with it.

Q   I would like to become more spiritual but have the feeling that I would have to get rid of my possessions which I love so much. Can you advise me?

A   It is natural to love our possessions. The problem begins when our possessions start to own us and not the other way round! Sometimes we have to let go of our possessions for the sake of our health but that has nothing to do with being spiritual.

Q   *How would someone who isn't psychic know when his or her hand was over a blockage, either in a vortex or a meridian line?*

A   Negative energy congestion produces heat. You would immediately feel it.

Q   *Would expanding the mind energy also remove these congestions in the body?*

A   Yes. By expanding the mind energy you lift the pressure off the brain and body and allow vital organs to vibrate again. An enormous amount of illness is due to pressure on these organs.

Q   *Would you say that more people have blockages in their bodies than not?*

A   Yes. I haven't met anyone yet who hasn't been blocked in some way or another. It is the type of life we all have to live nowadays. That is why the exercises in this book are so important.

Q   *Would you say these exercises are important even if one has no wish to become psychic?*

A   You are making a mistake that many people have

made before you and assuming that to be psychic is to be somehow abnormal or 'different'. Being psychic is normal – it is those who are not psychic who are abnormal. They have lost the instinct to survive. I am teaching all my readers to regain something they have lost – the most important part of themselves!

Self-Healing

Q   I have been practising self-healing ever since I read your first book and have been quite successful, but I still suffer bouts of asthma from time to time. How can I relieve the spasms?

A   An excellent way of relieving asthma attacks is to get someone to give you 'wheelbarrows'. That is, you get them to hold your legs up while you walk around the floor on your hands. If no-one is around to do this, lie down on the bed and hang your head over the side. These exercises force the oxygen to the brain.

Q   While self-healing, I have had a feeling of total euphoria. This is obviously because my mind energy has been released from the grip of my body. It seems to me that drug users could cut their drugs in this way. Do you agree?

A   I have taught mind exercises to people who take drugs, especially the great exercise of the Mind Medicine Room. By paying regular visits to this truly magical place to take their shots, some addicts have been able to come off drugs altogether while others have greatly reduced their intake.

Q   When I visit the Mind Medicine Room I find I only have to sit in the chair to feel better. Why is this?

A   Once you have established that this is the place where you get better and have complete faith in it, you will automatically have started a self-healing process within your body.

Q   Why is this?

A   Because the physical body is an extremely efficient factory and will produce whatever is needed given the help. 'Relaxation' is the secret word!

Q   I know your powers of clairvoyant diagnosis take in vitamins and minerals. Have you any message for slimmers?

A   Far too many people have messages for slimmers, and most of them contradict each other! I will merely say this. If you lose more than 1½lb a week, you will be poisoning yourself, because the fat content of the body absorbs all the poisons, sprays, etc., that you take in. DDT hasn't been used for years, yet people's bodies still contain it, and as the fat dissolves, the poison is released into the bloodstream and the person losing weight feels ill. You can lose little and regularly over, say, a year, and a lot of poison won't be suddenly released into the bloodstream.

Q   On one of my visits to my Mind Medicine Room

a man in a white doctor's coat suddenly appeared, put his hand on my head (I had a headache), and walked out of the door. The headache immediately disappeared. My arthritic knee was cured in the same way, by the appearance of this same 'doctor'! How can such a thing be explained? I certainly wasn't asleep at the time. Is it simply that I was relaxed?

A   When the mind energy is released and expanding, you can quite often see the energy dimension because you are part of it. There are many people in the next dimension who are helping us all the time. We are just not aware of them.

Q   *I think you could say 'the proof of the pudding is in the eating', so far as I am concerned. I visited you once because I was having epileptic fits and you cured me in one session. If the fits did come back at any time, how could I help myself?*

A   You could help yourself by visiting your Mind Medicine Room, sitting down in the chair and imagining a spirit doctor putting his or her hand on your head; also by visualizing broken links around your head being repaired.

Q   *My Medicine Room was so full of junk I had to visualize a second room. It proved beyond any show of doubt that my mind is a rubbish tip.*

A   An excellent piece of diagnosis! All you have to do now is to clear the junk out bit by bit until you can dispense with the second room. If you don't, you may need a third room!

Q I often feel dizzy and disoriented, but my doctor can find nothing wrong with me. Do you think I have a slipped mind energy?

A You can soon find out. Simply take a scarf, place it on your head, and pull it from one side to the other.

Q What does this do?

A The scarf becomes a magnet and will draw the mind energy back into position.

Q Why are you so sure that we can cure ourselves with the power of the mind?

A Because we can so easily kill ourselves by the same method. When a witch doctor 'points the bone', the victim goes away and dies. That is what certain peoples have been taught since birth.

Healing Others

Q While I was running my hands over the aura of one of my friends I felt something like an electric shock when I reached the bottom of her spine. She said that she always felt a pressure at that spot. I didn't know what to do so, remembering your lectures, I simply pulled out the energy. The tingling feeling left me and my friend's backache disappeared. Do you think I could become a healer?

A You already are a healer! We are *all* natural healers. Yet another gift most people have lost!

Q *I have tried healing my mother. She has told me she feels better but I feel nothing as yet. Is this right?*

A You don't have to feel anything. Simply have faith in what you are doing. Touch is the most important part of the exercise, and just letting the other person know that you really care.

Q *My father doesn't believe in 'psychics' and yet when he was in pain I put my hands on his head and the pain went. I have been following your exercises and it was quite easy to expand my mind so as to let in more life force and pass it on, but I am very angry that he still doesn't want to believe.*

A You cannot force your beliefs on others. By healing your father you have planted a seed, and in time it will grow. Just be happy that you were able to help him.

Q *In your book* MIND TO MIND *you described how, by projecting energy toward a plant, you were able to keep it alive for months without water. I tried this technique but after a week the plant was wilting and I had to water it. Yet I gave my mother some healing and she was cured. What went wrong in the case of the plant?*

A It is like life. You have to try, try and try again! Some of your experiments will fail but you may also find that you are able to do something quite unique that others can't. It depends on which wavelength you link up with. There are so many!

Q *I would love to become a vet but can't afford the training. Do you think I could become an animal healer?*

A If you have enough compassion and love for animals there is no reason why you shouldn't. Expansion of mind energy is a must for enhancing your awareness.

Q *Where can I receive the training?*

A I would try the exercises given on my tapes and in my books first (see the back of this book for details), and then practise on all the sick animals you can find. To be unique you have to stand alone.

Q *I would like to be able to link up with the wavelengths of animals. How can I do this?*

A All you have to do is have a very clear mental picture of the animal you wish to communicate with, then speak to it telepathically, but as directly as you would if you were speaking with your normal voice. If you want to get rid of animals or insects, just explain to them that you would not wish to hurt them so are asking them to go somewhere else where they will be safe. This works wonders with ants, moles, wasps, bees and other such creatures. If it is a domesticated animal with whom you wish to have better contact, then simply tell it that you are trying to understand its problem. Remember there are no language barriers in telepathic communication. Absent healing works wonders with animals. That is proof enough.

Absent Healing

Q *I am amazed at the improvement in my dog Cindy since absent healing began. How do you do it?*

A By mind-to-mind contact. Exactly as when I am giving absent healing to humans.

Q *I would like to give absent healing to friends. How do I start?*

A Have a clear picture of the person to whom the healing is being given. Ask for help for that person and then imagine a blue healing mist surrounding him or her.

Q *I'm afraid it won't work. I don't seem to have enough confidence in myself. What can I do to overcome this?*

A You must completely rid yourself of doubt, and *know* that you will succeed. Once you have had one success you will know you can do it.

Q *I sent some absent healing to my uncle by visualizing a strong white ray shining down on him.*

This helped him a great deal but, interestingly, he said he could see all the colours of the rainbow at about the same time. How could this be?

A   By raising your uncle's energies, especially mind energy, you enabled him to see into the energy dimension.

Q   How long should I give to absent healing for others?

A   No longer than five minutes. Remember the thought is the deed.

Q   Do you think that prayer is the same as absent healing?

A   It is similar. While giving absent healing one is thinking of the other person and his or her problem and carrying out certain exercises. But with prayer one usually asks God to do all the work. A combination of both would be much better!

Q   How would you give absent healing to someone with cancer tumours?

A   I would visualize the tumours breaking up or exploding and then pass a blue healing energy over the patient for peace of mind.

Q   How can I give healing to my mother who suffers from arthritis?

A   If you do not live near your mother just sit down

149

and have a clear picture of her in your mind. Then visualize a ray of light, preferably red, passing all over her and listen to the calcium deposits breaking up. It really works!

Q *My brother has epilepsy. Can I help him with absent healing?*

A Yes! Visualize all the broken links around his head linking up and completing the circuit.

Q *What links?*

A Around the body are links, probably electro-magnetic. In epilepsy some of these links are broken. This causes a short, similar to a fuse blowing in the house.

Q *My daughter has MS. How can I help her? She lives in South Africa.*

A If you sit down quietly and visualize a red glow around her body you will find this will energize her and give her more strength. This treatment has built up muscles in MS sufferers enabling them to walk a lot further than they did without the treatment.

Q *I have a friend who says 'It's fate' whenever anything horrible happens. Can you comment?*

A I think it is probably the only way she can cope with life. As I shall explain in the next chapter, I have always thought of fate as meaning 'From Another

Time Extracted'. It could be from other lifetimes. It is certainly not all bad. If something nice happens it is because you are receiving that which you have given out at some time. Universal Law dictates that what you give out will return in the fullness of time.

Q   Do you believe in fortune telling such as cards, hand reading, tarot, crystal balls, etc?

A   I used to be a hand analyst myself and it is a scientific study most of the time, but there are times when it is merely a focus for the psychic. This applies to everything else. If you are a good psychic you could give clairvoyance by studying a piece of string if you really thought it worked!

Q   Every time I step on a certain stone in my garden something strange happens. Why?

A   You are obviously quite psychic and because you expect it to happen, it does. This is quite common.

Q   I feel quite apprehensive about life, especially when I think about deeds returning to me. I don't know what I have done in previous lives, so how do I know what I am about to receive?

A   You don't. Neither do I. Life is a mixture of good and bad. All you can do is make sure you are not building up any more problems for yourself in the future. It's difficult being nice all the time but there are times when you could possibly give a lot of love to someone. That will be put to the credit side of your life's accounts. Remember, life is for living. Enjoy it. Live one day at a time.

Q   *I often hear the saying 'The sins of the fathers shall be visited upon the children.' What does this mean?*

A   I think I can explain it genetically. If your ancestors have been heavy drinkers then they would probably have had quite poor health, gout especially. Then they had children who inherited their genes, and so on. Eventually you will have inherited hundreds of diseases. All we can do is try to reverse the process by looking after ourselves and trying to change the genes in some way. A long process but each of us has to start somewhere.

If you look at the ecological state of the world today it will become quite clear what the saying means, though in a different way.

Q   *I have tried so hard to be positive, and yet negativity always seems to take over. Why?*

A   Sit down with a piece of paper and write a list of all the things you hate about life. Then write a list of all the things you like. Study them carefully. If the list of the things you dislike is longer than the list of those you like, then little by little you must change your life-style or you are, most definitely, on a losing streak. Nobody can be happy under these circumstances.

Q   Being positive all the time could make one into a bit of an idiot. Smiling at everyone, always being jolly. What do you think?

A   Idiots usually have a super life. They don't worry about anything. I think you may have the wrong idea about positivity. To be positive is to make sure that no-one is going to lead your life for you, it is to be independent as far as you are able, to look for the good things in life, to stop moaning and start doing, to make sure that you are going to be happy and healthy as far as you are able. If this means that you eventually smile at everyone instead of frowning, that's a bonus!

Q   What about being positively bad, is that good?

A   If it makes you happy without hurting anyone else, then so be it.

Q   I know it may sound awful, but I really like being negative. So why should I be positive?

A   Why should you indeed! Providing your negativity isn't creating health problems for yourself or others. The problem is that we can't live on an island and someone who is totally negative is probably making someone else as miserable as sin. Think about it!

Q   I have been taking your advice on positivity and have felt a lot better over the past six months. The trouble is that my husband is totally negative. What can I do for him?

A   Unfortunately there isn't much you can do for someone who wants to be negative. If your husband can see how much happier you are, he may want to change. If not, go out and about with friends who think like yourself. Enjoy life, that's what it's for.

Q   Someone once told me that negativity is a killer. What did she mean?

A   When you are negative the mind energy is sucked in and presses on the brain and body causing congestion in the body which leads to illness.

Q   Do you think that being positive all the time can cure illnesses?

A   It rather depends on what illness you are talking about. Being positive can certainly rid the body of pressures it could well do without when you are sick. Positivity through visualization can cure illnesses like cancer, and is an incredible tonic at all times.

Environment

Q   Why is it that suddenly we are living in a world that seems to be folding up? A few years ago no-one worried about the state of the rivers, seas, chicken farms and the like. I must say I was a lot happier then. Why worry now?

A   You are taking a very negative view of the whole

154

thing. People like myself have been trying to point out for decades the problems that were so obviously building up and, like yourself, nobody wanted to know. If something isn't done now our water will be undrinkable, Britain will be buried under concrete motorways, there will have to be more and more landfill sites to bury the mountains of plastic that won't rot, the whales will be extinct and so will the elephants. Cruelty to animals will become the norm. And the whole world will gradually die of diseases which will be far worse than Aids.

Q   Do you think there is any way we can counteract the terrible state of the ecology?

A   Most certainly! Make sure you write to your MP and press him or her to make sure that something is done about it. Or join the Green Party. They, at least, are desperately trying to help. You don't have to be politically minded, just care about the environment.

Q   I live near power lines and am invariably sick. As I can't sell my house (nobody wants to live near power lines), what can I do about it?

A   Try to spend as much time as you can out and about. This will probably make you feel better. Also, get together with your neighbours and petition the local Electricity Board to get the power lines put underground. Again, write to your MP. Keep trying.

Q   Why does it take so long for governments to do

anything about the ecology? Surely they must have been aware for some time of the problems that are facing us now?

A   The answer is big business. It also means spending a lot of money on cleaning up and governments can always find reasons for not becoming involved.

Q   Is the state of the environment as bad as people say it is?

A   I'm sorry to say this, but it is worse. If the real truth were to come out, it would be more than most people could take.

Q   Is there no hope at all?

A   There is always hope! If the whole world were to insist on change, governments would have to listen.

Mantra

Q   Can the practice of Mantras be dangerous in any way?

A   No, not at all. The nature of the sound is soothing and relaxing.

Q   Can children participate in chanting Mantras?

A   Yes. The earlier you can encourage children to participate the better. It helps with concentration by directing their attention to the task in hand.

Q Is it good for parents and children to chant Mantras together?

A It is good for the whole family because it draws them together emotionally and brings a greater understanding to everyone involved.

Q When should one practise?

A At any time of the day or night when it is quiet.

Q Are Mantras good for curing physical ailments?

A Yes they are. The vibrations created through using sound frequencies enable the body to self-heal.

Q Can Mantras benefit insomniacs?

A They are especially beneficial to them.

Q Do you have to believe in the Hindu religion to practise Mantras?

A It is not specifically a religious practice so you certainly do not have to belong to any particular religion. Having said that, religions all over the world do practise Mantras for peace and spirituality.

Q What changes should I be looking for if I practise Mantras?

A You will be aware that your basic nature has changed. Material possessions will not be so important to you and you will feel more loving towards others. Your health also will most certainly improve, especially your breathing.

Q *Can I teach myself or do I have to go to a qualified teacher?*

A With the help of tapes you can certainly teach yourself. In the privacy of your own home you can become familiar with the sound of your own voice and your mental and physical reactions to it.

Q *Do I need to know music or be able to sing in tune?*

A No! Definitely not. Vibration is within yourself and your voice will produce the vibrations that are best suited to you. Remember, we are all unique!

Q *Can a Mantra be any word?*

A In theory Mantras were always Sanskrit words meaning peace, forgiveness, love, thankfulness. In fact, you could chant any positive word and you would receive the same benefits. Mantra is energy of the most powerful kind and attracts like energies.

Part Two

LIVING

Nine

HINTS FOR A HAPPY LIFE

How happy is he born and taught
That serveth not another's will
Whose armour is his honest thought
And simple truth his utmost skill.

Sir Henry Wotton (1568-1639),
The Character of a Happy Life

In the first part of this book I have been teaching you the technique of healing yourself and others through the magic principle of MIND ENERGY. But healing is not concerned with the needs of the body alone. It is also concerned with peace of mind. What is the point of being 100 per cent physically fit if the spirit is restless, dissatisfied and disturbed, if you are nasty to other people and a nuisance to yourself? In offices, railway carriages, wherever people are jammed together, you only have to look around you and listen to the conversations to realize that half the world is fed up with itself. How sad – and how much sadder when anger, grumbling and discontent penetrate, as all too often they do, into the one place where harmony and good fellowship should reign – that is, the home. Here is negativity on the rampage, negativity at its most lethally destructive. Escape from it while you can!

This next section is concerned with teaching you how to live so that you can continue the work of expanding your mind energy by expelling the poison of negativity for ever and enthroning the positive in its place. But such an achievement will not be brought about in a day. Nor will all of us accomplish it at the same speed. For just as we are all born with different physical potentialities, so are we all born with different legacies from the past, in the form of our temperaments, surroundings and family influences. In other words, each of us has a different hand of cards to play. We call that our fate. But what is fate?

FATE

Ninety per cent of the population have no idea what fate means. When something bad befalls us we say: 'What have I done to deserve this?' Unless your understanding is better than this, you will always blame someone or something else, never yourself, and call it 'fate'! So I will make the explanation easy for you.

F - A - T - E : From Another Time Extracted. All the good and bad things we have done, both in this life and in our previous existences — for remember, the mind is everlasting because energy is indestructible — have to be paid for in the end. What you give out will come back tenfold and more. In a past life you may have been a saint, but in this life, perhaps because of the circumstances of your birth, you are a criminal – or just a creep! Yet others envy your material assets, your luxurious life style. They say: 'Why should such an appalling person be entitled to such a good deal?' What that person has done is to reap the rewards of a good life the last time round. That, precisely, is FATE – From Another Time Extracted! That, and no more. So it is up to such a person to mend his or her bad ways now. Otherwise the universal computer will get to work and in a future existence you will be back to square one.

Remember, in your life or lives, past, present and to come, whatever you give out you will get back. There is true justice in this. It is the law of the universe and there is no hiding from it for any of us. I have seen good and bad deeds return in the space of a few days, or, at other times, in a few years. There is no special time scale for retribution and rewards, only lessons for us to learn when the time is right for us to receive them. That is why we should take steps to moderate our excesses and errors.

So-called 'saintly' behaviour is boring: we are given our lives to enjoy. But the other side of the coin is also boring, with its lack of compassion and spirituality. It can also manifest unbelievable cruelty both mental and physical. Walking the middle path will give us a happy, normal life – no small achievement in itself. If we can notch up extra points for compassion and spirituality, well and good, but only if our feelings are genuine and from the heart. All things are known. You may not be scoring as many points as you think.

INHERITANCE

Affecting us also, but in a rather more obvious way, is our ancestry. All of us suffer, or benefit as the case may be, from the way in which our ancestors, grandparents and parents lived. We have inherited their genes, and the health or otherwise of our genetic structure is passed down to us from them and is outside our control. What they did to their bodies directly affects ours, and what we do to ours will affect those of our children. If anyone gets it wrong, abnormalities and diseases multiply all along the line, and these will show up earlier and earlier in young lives. Conversely, if we turn our behaviour around we can arrest the downward spiral, our children will be born fitter, and their genetic structure will be altered for the better this time. If we behave well, that is another way of saying that we are using our mind energy well; if badly, then the reverse. It is never too late, but the greatest blessing we can confer on our children is to train them properly from birth. Before they can speak they can feel and therefore automatically will already be picking up vibrations from their parents' energy counterparts and minds.

SPIRITUALITY

What you achieve with your body and your mind depends on you, and the result is your spirituality

– so don't let that high-sounding word throw you. So many people associate it exclusively with religion in the narrow sense. That is not correct. To be spiritual is to be part of the universal energy. Whether you combine religion and spirituality is up to you. Spirituality means 'pertaining to the spirit'; spirit is essence; essence is energy. That is the best explanation. What we must never forget is that, however we play with words, when it comes to leading our lives we have freedom of thought, word, and deed. That is, we have choice, and the responsibility for the choices we make is ours and ours alone.

But what are we to do to make sure we are in a position to make our choices positively and well? The answer, once more, is, by expanding our mind energy. There are all sorts of common-sense ways in which we can do this and the rest of this chapter, and the next, will be aimed at suggesting some of those which I think are the most important, and the attitudes without which we cannot expect to get by. And first, a virtue which is welcome everywhere and always – humour.

HUMOUR

Having a sense of humour is one of the greatest gifts that can be bestowed on us. Without humour life is a nightmare. The ability to make people laugh makes you automatically a member of the healing league, for it is the greatest healer of all.

I have this ability and have used it all my life, but especially in my healing practice.

No matter how ill my patients may be, I know if I can make them smile there is more chance of a cure. If I can make them laugh, that's even more of a bonus.

Laughter releases pent-up emotion. By dislodging congestive energies it takes the pressure off the major organs, allows the body to function and can instantly cure malfunction. Negativity and despair fly out of the window. Colours are brighter, even the weather in England becomes tolerable! It can even restrain you from polishing off your children, your spouse and your pets, in that order. It can't be bad!

For that reason, comedians are among the greatest healers of all. I have studied the auras of audiences in theatres and the effect comedians have on them is absolutely magnificent.

Before the performance begins the energies are normal; our energy line, when we are reasonably healthy, is about one to one and half inches around the body, as I have said. During the performance, especially if the comedian is good, the energies are sparkling with colour and life and blending one with another, until the theatre or hall is filled with energy (usually blue, I find!) – a sea of energy that helps also to stimulate the performer, for we all draw from each other.

The reason for this, as I have also explained earlier (see chapter Two), is that the chakras, those rotating vortices of energy, are being stimulated. The life force we draw in dislodges negative congestion within the body, thus enabling the energies to flow and expand.

All artists, not only comedians, but opera singers and all other performers, feel this sea of energy when the audience is with them. It creates total rapport. They also fail miserably when the audience is against them because anger, boredom or just plain lack of interest will cause the congestive energies to block even more and thus prevent the vortices from drawing in life force to stimulate the energy system. So the auras fail to expand and there is no linking up. Without the sea of energy the artist cannot be stimulated and 'dies', as stage parlance has it. In other words, the performance is always very much below par and on occasion a total disaster.

We desperately need both our own humour and the humour of others. Without it we become isolated and our health deteriorates mentally as well as physically.

Laughter is the beginning of all healing. Everyone feels the better for having had a good laugh. If you find that laughter has gone from your life, you must make every effort to bring it back in again, even if that means seeking out the company of people you don't specially like but who, for some reason, make you laugh. Buy videos that make you laugh.

Watching them will be as good as a real healing session!

SEEKING KNOWLEDGE

Now here is another and most valuable way of expanding your mind energy by disciplining your mind. For remember, as I have said: *an undisciplined mind will always be the servant of a disciplined mind.*

The subject matter you choose is not important. What is important is to spend some time each day acquiring it. In this way the mind energy expands, taking the pressure away from the physical body and linking up to the Universal Mind, that vast sea of information that can be tapped merely by concentration. If you study your subject well you will find this linking up becoming easier and easier as the months go by. Moreover, by spending a certain amount of your time day-dreaming (yes, day-dreaming!) about your subject your intuition will become second to none.

If you find studying difficult, start by timing yourself and switch off after ten minutes. Do not allow yourself any more time that day. You will find after a few days that because your time is limited you will be anxious not to want to waste a moment of it. Then you will want to extend the limit to fifteen minutes and so on until your interest has been stimulated to such a degree that you will be reluctant to finish at all, and will wish your studies could continue indefinitely. And while all this is happening, one remarkable change will have taken place. You will discover that you have not had time to think about yourself at all!

Studying for long periods may make you feel tired. What it will not do is to make you feel bored and negative. That is the biggest bonus of all.

Are you one of those who feel discouraged and disappointed because you lack what is known as 'a good education'? If so, I sympathize – I started like that myself. But I can tell you, it's never too late, there are always opportunities, and besides, though higher education and a university degree are a wonderful advantage for some, they are by no means the best thing for everybody. Being 'clever' is not the same as being intelligent or even sensible. Some really brainy people are exceptionally silly, some too are exceptionally unreceptive to unfamiliar ideas, and there are loads of men and women with good academic degrees who, as the saying goes, couldn't even run a whelk stall!

As I described in *Mind to Mind*, I grew up during the Second World War. I had a rough time of it – in fact, for over a year, I was half starved. No chance for me of a degree from Oxford or Cambridge! So I have had to teach myself, and I have thoroughly enjoyed doing so.

I have been a bookworm all my life, and everything I read and everything I learn really means something to me. Jung, Laurens van der Post and

Bertrand Russell are three authors from whom I have learned to write with simplicity.

Perhaps you are young, still in your teens or only just out of them, and perhaps your school results were not as good as they might have been, either because you were a bit of a late developer, or because you had troubles at home – or because you were being a rebel! Again, don't worry. Just pick up the bits, get on with things, and be positive. About this vital positivity you will find more in the next chapter.

If you are unhappy at work or in your private life, give thought to the situation but do not worry about it. Turn your mind to other things. Again by reversing the mind energy you cause the brain and body to react and are able to tackle your problems in a more relaxed way.

There is an answer to every problem but very often we have to wait some time before we can see the wood for the trees. By worrying and causing pressure to build up on the brain we merely cloud the issue. But controlling our mind energy is the way to control our life.

GETTING BACK TO NATURE

Next I come to a subject very close to my own heart. No matter what our occupations may be, getting back to nature is an essential step towards health. We all need spiritual sustenance and to deny ourselves this leads to mental and physical illness.

To be able to look into the distance, expand your mind energy and become aware of the link-up with other energy fields gives you an incredible boost. Again, you have this wonderful feeling of release and letting go of tension.

If you are unable to get out of your house through illness, or escape for whatever reason from a congested urban area, don't despair. We all have a mind, we can expand our mind energy, and by thought we can travel anywhere. The thought is the deed. Just sit quietly, close your eyes and think yourself anywhere in the world you would like to be.

First of all, reinforce the sensation of being there. If it is by the sea listen to the waves crashing against the rocks, feel the spray on your face, feel the sand between your toes as you walk barefoot along the beach, feel the sun warming your skin, your face. With practice these sensations will become so intense that the scenery will begin to impress itself on your mind and the pictures will become totally real.

Much more real, in fact, than the pictures on your television screen, and much better for you! All of us can benefit from this travelling by thought, but none more, perhaps, than those who are ill in hospital, or lying sick at home. For them it is a real tonic.

But perhaps you don't feel you're much good at

letting go. You don't? Well, have you every really tried? Have you ever . . . ? Have you ever . . . ?

HAVE YOU EVER . . . ?

Have you ever sat beside a stream on a hot summer's day watching the water rippling over stones which look like bright, shiny gems? Or suddenly glimpsed a large fish silvery in the sunlight?

Have you ever sat in a field of ripe corn watching it sway with the breeze and experienced the mystical feeling of belonging as your energies merge with your surroundings and you sway back and forth for a magical moment in time?

Have you ever sat on top of a mountain breathing the cool air and feeling its cleanness as your lungs fill with this magic substance?

Have you ever sat in a wood watching the rabbits as they run around, heads popping up from their burrows, careful, watchful, as their babies take their first tremulous steps, then, finding their feet, start to hop about with joy?

Have you ever waited for hours beside a badger run hoping to see that beautiful black and white head appear?

Have you ever spent time watching birds making their nests and waiting patiently for their babies to hatch out until – probably while you are not looking – the chicks leave the nest for the first time?

Have you ever sat with your back to an old oak tree to absorb the energy of the tree and become one with it, listening to the unspoken yet powerful vibrations that are continually emanating from it? Tree talk!

Have you ever lain on the grass, listened to it and heard it growing?

Have you ever talked to your flowers and plants? Then it's high time you did! Unlike Prince Charles, I don't risk being laughed at in public when I tell you they really do listen.

Have you ever swum in the sea with the dolphins or talked to the seals? Or sunbathed on a deserted beach listening to the cry of the seagulls overhead and the calming sound of the sea as it washed the shore?

Have you ever lain down on the lawn and stared at the sky on a bright summer's day, watching globules of energy exploding like bright, minute pin-heads?

If you have never experienced any of these things, or not enough of them, you can start now!

When you go out into the country for the day, or on holiday, feel at one with your surroundings, become aware of the natural vibrations and the energy of nature. Choose a quiet place where you can do the balloon exercises (see pages 51–62) to expand your mind and you will begin to experience that magical feeling of oneness with nature.

While you are still up in your balloon feel the material you are wearing, the floor you are sitting on, the wood of your chair. They are telling you something. Everything has a story. The energy of the person who made the chair will always be there and the energy of the original tree will always be there. Energy in any form can never be destroyed.

Or lean against the trunk of a tree and listen. You will be surprised at the different vibrations you will pick up. Or if there are seagulls overhead listen to them – feel as though you are flying around with them, that you are one of them.

Maybe your balloon will take you to the mountain top and you will feel the cool mountain breeze as it brushes against your face. Being at one with nature is our only chance of survival. We have ignored its language for too long and we cannot afford to do so any more. If we had listened carefully long ago most of the terrible things that have happened in this earth would never have occurred.

Knowing needs no language at all. Knowing is a feeling of right or wrong, of being happy or unhappy, of being confident or lacking in confidence. It is a sense of being, and when you know, there is no going back. You will always know. This sounds mystical perhaps. Well, it *is* mystical. For the mystique of being at one with nature will take you over, and what better way could there be to live than by nurturing and caring for everything that makes this planet beautiful?

If you are unable to go out for any reason, don't worry. Wood, mountain top and sea shore can all be visited in your mind. Your mind energy can take you wherever you wish to go; all you have to do is lose yourself within your imagination and your mind will expand to reach the farthest places on earth if you so wish. It is a type of astral travel, if you like, but travel that you can discipline and command and not the sort of butterfly-minded existence over which you have no control. You can experience everything: there is no need to travel physically at all.

Enjoy your travels and your expanding awareness. In so doing you will also find the nature of your being. But now for two qualities so crucial to that being's health that I shall write about them in separate chapters.

Ten

HONESTY

Truth is too simple for us; we do not like those who unmask our illusions.

Ralph Waldo Emerson (1803–82)

We all tell lies. Sometimes they are little white lies. Sometimes they are large ones. Sometimes they are told with the best intentions, to save somebody's feelings. Sometimes they are told out of malice and to cause mischief. But lying is something we have all been guilty of, and that is why I think this chapter is so important.

As children we become used to hearing our parents tell us lies, either because they think they will be for our good or because the pressures of parenthood have become too much for them and they are taking the easy way out. Not unnaturally we grow up with the same bad habits and these habits are strengthened by use. In the end we become oblivious of the fact that we are indeed liars – some of us very practised liars!

This is a tragic state of affairs because lying corrodes our spirit. It wounds the mind energy, which is the deepest part of us, so when we lie we are inflicting a wound on ourselves. Sometimes lying makes us physically dizzy, even ill. That is because the mind energy has become lopsided.

But however deep the habit of lying has grown in

you, there is still time to change. Maybe you will have to tell white lies; they are sometimes inevitable. But telling unnecessary lies is simply a bad habit, and it can cause immense damage.

For years I have been listening to the problems caused by lies and have seen the irreparable damage that they can produce; and I too have suffered when people have lied to me. Let's face it, lying is an abominable habit.

How can you change? First, you must promise yourself that you *will* change. You must stop lying to yourself. And having made that promise, you must keep it. Tell yourself that you will make the change little by little, so that it isn't too drastic. After all, you have got to retrain yourself, and retraining oneself is never easy. You don't want too much pressure coming into your life all at once. We can all do without that!

If a friend asks you a simple question try to answer it as truthfully as you can without causing hurt. Start with half a lie if necessary – at least you will be halfway there!

Have the courage of your convictions. People usually resort to lying because they lack the courage to tell the truth. But when you lie to someone you can bet your bottom dollar that you will be found out: someone else will put that person wise – and with imaginative additions! Then you will cause more hurt than if you had told the truth in the first place, particularly if the person you have lied to is a friend. It really is a vicious circle.

Telling the truth is not easy. Every day we all have to tell white lies for one reason or another. But wouldn't it be super if you could cut your output of lies by 75 per cent? All right, you may lose a few friends for a while, but you will undoubtedly make new ones who will appreciate your integrity. And believe me, your old friends will come back in the end too – because now they will know that they can trust you to tell them the truth.

Always be sympathetic. Never embellish something that you know will hurt, even in its simplest form. Try to sweeten the pill with a little philosophy – it will help you also to see the world in a different light.

When we lie, we also damage our own psyche. Lying is an attack on our own spirituality which will come back in time and force us to face ourselves at a time when we are most vulnerable.

Perhaps the saddest thing of all about lying is that once we have been caught out, the person we have deceived may never trust us again. I think that is very sad, because many liars are quite nice people most of the time. When you have lost a friend through your cowardice in telling a lie there may not be much you can do about it. But at least you can impress new people who enter your life with your honesty, sympathy and integrity.

Never make promises you know you can't fulfil. If you have any doubt about fulfilling a promise, then just say you will do your best to carry it out but on no account promise faithfully that you will do so.

People in business lie to each other all the time; they seem to think that if they don't, they will fail to get to the top, or even be sacked! It becomes such a habit that they no longer know they are lying and really believe their own publicity! Top men get their subordinates to lie for them, and so it goes on. When you think about it, what a terrible way to live! Why not be less successful and do without the trimmings in your life that you don't really need? That way, at least you will be able to hold up your head.

Do you really need the big house, the expensive car, the designer clothes, and all the rest? Who are you trying to impress? The only people you will impress will be those who desperately want to be like you. They are people who have, like yourself, lost their spiritual path and can no longer enjoy the simple things in life. They don't find these things exciting enough.

If you really want to change and lead a more respectable life, even though it may not be such an outwardly successful life, then reduce your overheads, look for a smaller house, buy a smaller car. Above all, enjoy your family and friends.

There is nothing more joyful than spending time with people you love and care for. Giving instead of receiving, especially giving of yourself, your emotions. Allow your children to become part of your emotional life instead of your materialistic life. Tell them that they will have more of your company and fewer empty goodies. I know which most of them would rather have!

If children have been thoroughly spoiled and would rather have the goodies, then you will have to re-educate them and teach them to accept less. It will be mainly your fault that they are what they are! Teach them about nature, the spirit of the sea, the mountains, the forests. Take them to stay in an area of natural beauty so that you and they may recapture what you have lost.

It will be like being reborn. Born again naturalists! You will see your surroundings with new eyes, the grass will look greener, the trees will look alive and have characters of their own, the flowers will have brighter hues and finding wild orchids, bluebells, primroses, wild daffodils, honeysuckle, wild black-berries, sloes, rosehips and herbs will make you realize what you have been missing. Your children will be healthier, the whole family will be healthier. Instead of continually worrying about finance you will be able to sleep at night.

If you are a townie go and sit in your local park. If there isn't one near you then take a bus ride to one of the big parks that are always filled with beautiful flowers. Breathe deeply. Fill your lungs with air and your blood with oxygen. All right, you will breathe in fumes as well, but you are doing that anyway!

What a different sort of life you could have just by cutting out the lies!

We all suffer from the lies that political parties hand out to us – the promises rarely, if ever, fulfilled, the U-turns, the contradictions. And these are the people we were taught to look up to because they knew best! How stupid we were to believe them and how let down we feel by our own stupidity.

History as far back as you can go tells of the lies and fabrications of governments and heads of state, yet we still listen to what they say. Not only do they lie to the public but they lie to themselves, their friends and their colleagues, and what is more they believe what they are saying because lying has become to them a natural way of life. If one political party can pull a fast one over the other that's considered very smart and everyone has a great laugh. But these are the people who are running the country, so it's not such a laugh really. In fact, it is tragic.

Perhaps one day a party will emerge that will not only teach us to live more simply and get back to nature but make sure there will still be a planet for our children to enjoy. Such a party will have to be closely involved with the spirit of nature because we cannot exist without being aware of the great Universe of Energy that creates the whole.

In the end, when you lie you are only hurting yourself. Whatever you give out will come back to you tenfold and more, no matter how long it takes. You can hide behind lies for only so long. Believe me, they will return.

In the course of my career, and particularly since the publication of my first book, *Mind to Mind*, I have been asked to do many things, which could bring me more immediate attention than I have now. I have refused, because I would be lying to myself if I pretended that I enjoyed doing them. My motto has always been 'To thine own self be true'. It isn't such a bad motto when you think about it because in the end we all have to live with ourselves.

When it comes to being truthful about our emotional lives this can and does present tremendous problems. But living a lie can also cause hurt, and terrible physical and mental problems, to both sides. I know, because as a healer I have seen it all! Practically 85 per cent of my patients have emotional problems of one sort or another. About 70 per cent are living with people they dislike and with whom, every day, they face the same package of deceit and lies. This situation destroys them. It is much better to cut your losses and live in a bed-sit than go through life being made physically and mentally ill.

Sometimes a separation is good for both sides because only then do they realize what they are missing. You have to have the courage of your convictions and courage is what most people lack.

Of course, if you can, it is much better to start talking, maybe for the first time in your relationship. Start by refusing to lie about the small things. If there is love and respect between you then it will surface. If there isn't, you had better face up to the fact, even if this means losing out on the material side of life. What is more important, material things or your self-respect and health? Do you really love your inanimate possessions so much? What are they giving you, as a person? Not much!

I have heard many men and women say they

would dearly love to leave their partners but those partners are so sensitive – the separation would kill them. If your partner is as sensitive as all that, then he or she will already have picked up the fact that you are not happy. An atmosphere will have built up that anybody can sense. Do you really want to live in that sort of stifling atmosphere for the rest of your life? It is much better to be sympathetic, loving and truthful.

I am sure that many marriages and relationships could be saved by being more truthful. Would it not be better to be able to confide in your partner in the knowledge that you would be understood, than live a life of domestic lies while spending negative hours burdening your best friends with accounts of your unhappiness?

Let me repeat. Start by telling the truth about the little things in life. You will then find a natural progression to the big things. Rome wasn't built in a day and neither are relationships.

No matter how much in love two people are when they start living together, the time will come when they have to settle for less romance and attention, especially when children arrive. There's nothing like children for putting an end to spare time, sound sleep, and a peaceful sexual relationship!

Sex! That is something the whole world lies about! Let me put your mind at rest about some of the things to do with it – I hasten to add, not all from my own experience!

Sex isn't as incredible as most people would have

us believe. Many people have lied to me about their sexual prowess and I have wondered why they bother – after all, I *am* clairvoyant! When you think about it, you don't fall in love – and I do mean love and not lust – with a person's physical attributes but with their mind, their loving nature, their ability to make you laugh, their sensitivity, their warmth, their love of nature or animals or other human beings – their love of everything and everybody in fact but especially because of the rapport they have with you. Then at some time you sleep together. The first time you have sex it can be a dismal failure and very often is. You are both new to each other and because other people have filled you with stories of their own incredible sexual relationships, most of which are probably fictitious, you think you have been let down.

Loving is the most important part of a sexual relationship – if that is missing, then the rest will never be right. It will very soon end, because that kind of relationship is very easy to find elsewhere. But if the loving is there then everything will come right in time, even if you are not well matched physically or other things of that sort are not perfect. It really doesn't matter because there are so many ways in which you can please someone you love. The worst harm you can bring to a sexual relationship is to lie about it – to pretend that you are enjoying it when you are not. White lies are permissible so that feelings shall not be hurt, but gradually you must come round to saying what you would like and asking your partner what he or she would like. Break down any barriers you have. You never know, it may surprise you how inventive you both can be! Don't continue to allow any behaviour you find abhorrent; your partner may not realize that that is how you feel and years later may be terribly upset to find out what you really thought. This can cause a lot of bitterness right at the end of people's lives.

There are many ways in which both partners can have a happy physical relationship. You may not both like all the same things but there is no reason at all why you should not please each other in different ways. Be inventive in a sensitive way. You will be surprised at how much more enjoyable your life can be. Above all talk to each other. Communication is the key word, especially when it comes to sex. Try it, it really works. So much better than living a lie.

It is lack of communication that leads to adultery, a state of affairs that hurts everyone involved. The majority of people do not want to hurt anyone. They simply want a truthful relationship with no barriers, and having found one they discover that it is spiritually rewarding. Just think of it – to share your life with someone with whom you have no secrets. It is mind-boggling! Unfortunately with adultery everyone gets hurt, and because most people hang on to their possessions no matter how miserable their lives may be, they usually return to their partners. In most cases, materialism wins out over love, make no mistake about it. That is why we have to examine our own motives all the time and not fall into the pit that has swallowed up so many before us.

If you are asked a question, think first and give yourself time to answer. Pausing for a second can actually prevent you from lying. Maybe you will find that you can actually tell the truth. It is amazing how easy it is. Indeed, eventually you may become hooked on it !

The object of this chapter has been to plant the seed of truth. I have not given examples of all the sorts of lies that can be told, or of the motives behind them. We all know the lies that we ourselves tell, and perhaps we think some of them are justified. If so, that is a matter between us and our own consciences. But in our hearts we all know that what I have been saying is true – that there is a better way of leading our lives.

Telling the truth means becoming more spiritual. But beware, this means change. It is not so easy to lead the spiritual life, but the exercises and advice throughout this book will all have helped because they too will have been building up your spiritual side and giving you strength to face your challenges.

Instinctively, you will begin to feel that lying to others is wrong. Progress in this will present you with many hurdles to jump, but believe me, when it comes to the last one or two, you will find that there is someone or something there to help you over them. You will be seen to have deserved it. As you struggle, you will probably think that there is no help there at all, but looking back as you grow older you will see that it has all been worthwhile. Your character will have been strengthened and so will your mind energy – that power house which is enabling you to live the life you wish without doing harm to other people.

It is amazing how strong we become by overcoming obstacles. So stop lying, start living!

Eleven

POSITIVITY

> Never say any man is hopeless, because he only
> represents a character, a bundle of habits, and these
> can be checked by new and better ones.
>
> Vivekananda

I have spoken a great deal in this book about the
need for positivity – how this attitude is essential
if we are to expand our mind energy and how its
opposite, negativity, reduces it. Here is an example
of positivity at its most spectacular.

The scene is my flat on the outskirts of London,
a few years ago, at the time when I was living and
working there. The time is 9 a.m., and I am waiting
to receive my first client. She is a new client, so I
have never met her before, and know little about her
reasons for wanting to come to see me. Sharp on the
hour I hear a car draw up outside the building and
I wait for the bell to ring.

No bell! Ten minutes later, still no bell! I open the
door and look out to see what is happening.

The flat is approached by a flight of concrete steps.
As I look down them I see a lady crawling up, one
step at a time, dragging a pair of lifeless legs behind
her. 'Hi!' she calls out to me. 'I'm Pat. I'll be with
you in a minute.'

I can hardly believe it. This morning I had woken up feeling tired and out of sorts, reluctant to embark on the labours of another day. Now my negative attitude has vanished – in fact, I feel thoroughly ashamed of it. And looking into Pat's smiling face and twinkling eyes I realize at once that there will be no need to give her the little book on positivity that I hand out to most of my clients. Pat has enough positivity to fill several books of her own!

Pat crawled up those steps once a week for a month. Then she tottered up them, using the hand-rail. Finally, after three months, she was *running* up them, completely cured. But without her contribution of positivity and self-help, I would never have been able to heal her.

While healing Pat I studied her mind energy and was amazed at how brilliant and expansive it was. The fact that her body was crippled didn't matter – her thoughts were positive. Her mind energy was linked up with the cosmos and this power, thus transmitted, was stimulating the energy counterpart and the vortices. Pat's courage and determination, by expanding her mind energy, had won the day. Without them, she would probably still be on all fours.

I stood there thinking about my own feelings that morning, how tired I had felt, longing for a day off, and then looked at Pat completing her mammoth tasks. No matter how feeble you may feel, if someone told you tomorrow that you would be losing the use of your legs I guarantee the first thing you would do would be to walk miles to

189

prove the prediction wrong and boost your own morale.

Remember, anything is possible if you want it enough. Think how much we could achieve if we made the same effort while healthy as Pat did while she was ill. With a positive approach illnesses can be avoided and success is inevitable.

How does it feel when you are positive? There is one word for it: powerful. Why do you feel powerful? Because the thought process has reversed the direction of your mind energy which is now expanding, linking up to the cosmic forces. The more positive you are the more energy you are absorbing.

For many years I have studied the form of athletes. From the beginning of their training they are channelled to win. They push themselves and pit themselves against near-impossible odds. There is no thought of defeat, and if for one moment they do give in to that negative emotion they lose verve, electricity and drive, until, once again, they reverse the thought and become positive. Why? Because they lose that vital link with life force energies.

If we know about these energies we are already way ahead of our colleagues and competitors.

Positivity! Its rewards are immense in every walk of life. Are you working to be a painter? If so, you will be starting to see, with your mind's eye, colours so bright that they might have been sprinkled with stardust. Their beauty will be exceptional, your perception of them extra keen, the finished product a delight to the soul. Never again will you have to sit staring at an empty canvas, wondering where to start. Your subject will reveal itself because you will have linked up with like minds, and inspiration will be the result. New visions will come to you with as much ease and speed as if you had just drawn back a curtain. Insights formerly hidden from you will suddenly be revealed. If this sounds far-fetched it is because you have never really linked up with another dimension. You have been too 'earthed' and have sadly been missing out on the truly great experiences – those of the mind.

Perhaps you are a musician or singer. The vibrations produced by playing or singing are the easiest way to open up and expand the mind energy. Linking up with spiritual sources is automatic but to become a genius you need to know your subject in depth. Only then can you forget the mechanics of performance. This also applies to mind expansion. Eventually you will be able to forget the exercises – that is, the mechanics.

I have known musicians and singers who have been brilliant technicians but have completely lacked soul. They failed to make the grade as professionals. I have also heard musicians and singers, especially pop groups, who are so awful it is painful to listen to them yet who have made it to the top. All right, this may be partly because young people, reared on television, have too little opportunity to listen to beautiful music. They have grown up with so much shouting and screaming that they truly believe that this constitutes good music. Their musical education is nil. Yet the pop groups they love would never succeed unless they – or their managers! – were driven by positivity.

This goes even more for the great age of jazz, the dazzling musicians of Harlem in its heyday, the black singers second to none. Most of them learned their music as young children singing in church, and that taught them the most valuable lesson of all. That you have to have soul, which means positivity at a deep level.

Do you aspire to be a writer? Then words will flow from you with hardly a single conscious thought. Like attracts like. Your mind will attract other minds of a similar stamp that will impress themselves upon it and strengthen it. From this linking up will emerge one single thought – and what a thought it will be! You will have at your command a powerhouse of information and a straight line to the Universal Mind. Who knows, you may write a bestseller one day!

There are lots of things to write about, too. Not all books need to be highbrow novels, or heavy historical studies. The secret is to have one subject on which you are truly expert and to learn to expound it in a simple yet imaginative style. It is also worth writing just for private circulation – that is, for distribution among your family and friends. Too few chronicles are written these days – good ones, that is. An awful lot of people feel they have no roots because there are no family diaries. Why not work on your family history, with whatever oral memories or written materials are to hand, and see how far you can get with it? It will take you into all sorts of interesting byways – and perhaps reveal a few skeletons in the cupboard which great-great-grandfather would have preferred to keep locked away! Even more privately, you can look back on your own past, candidly recording your former tears and fears to increase your self-knowledge and your understanding of your own children. Self-examination, so long as it is kept within bounds, can be wonderfully therapeutic.

When I think of the many young people who are unemployed and do nothing but laze around all the time or dream of being rock musicians and singers because they believe it will bring them instant fame and money, I cannot help feeling what a terrible waste of youth and energy it all is. Every person has a genetic, inherited skill. So why not use yours to meet a general need – at the same time as satisfying some of your own inmost desires?

People today are becoming sick of the plastic age in all its forms and teenagers are just the people to relearn the old crafts. They are young, they are untrammelled, and some of them have started already. Never mind the rock idols. You can become just as famous, though your fame may be long-term rather than instantaneous. Everyone is looking for houses of character, whether old or just well built, furniture as solid as that of a hundred years ago and crafted with the same loving skill. The beautiful wrought iron gates at the entrance to properties have been replaced by mass-produced shams, old bricks that had a rosy glow and were made to last for ever have been banished in favour of pock-marked modern products that one hopes will not last at all.

The beauty of a landscaped garden and the skills of the old gardeners! What wonderful people they were! What beautiful clay pots could once be bought and filled with flowers to brighten some modest back yard. What delight to have a home that was not just an empty box but a place full of hidden corners and irregular designs which children as well as their parents would savour for the rest of their lives. The once forgotten art of making musical instruments is now coming back. What pleasure to play an instrument you have made yourself, to hang a picture on the wall that is all your own work. You never know – someone may offer to buy it!

Becoming an apprentice to a goldsmith or silversmith is also a modern possibility. So is learning a foreign language, or learning your own well enough to earn your living as a journalist.

But most people have now gone beyond the years of teenage dreaming and most people are not artists. Most people, in fact, have to do ordinary, everyday jobs – jobs that can be so boring that they drive you nearly out of your mind. What do you do then to improve yourself and expand your mind energy?

Don't worry! I have lived through that situation myself and I can suggest one answer at least. If you can't change your job, start doing it so well that within its limits, it becomes almost an art form. Write beautifully, type beautifully, speak beautifully, make sure you do everything as perfectly as you possibly can. This will give you pride in your job, however dull, and being positive you will be attracting positive energies that will keep you going and give you a feeling of peace. It really works, believe me! When you go home make sure that you take time out to pursue a hobby that will give you pleasure and something to look forward to as well. Don't let negativity become a part of your life because if you do you will certainly become a loser.

Then let your ambitions run free. There are hobbies that can become professions. Perhaps handicrafts attract you. Perhaps you would like to know how to weave or make up jumpers with exotic, foreign designs. Or maybe you would like to be another Anita Roddick going all over the world looking for natural substances to use for making your own cosmetics. After all, women have made their own beauty aids since the beginning of time. Now we all rely on others to do it for us.

Forestry is another fantastic job, planting and looking after trees and forests. What a lovely thought! Perhaps you would like to build bridges in primitive places. Or become an explorer or climber. Everest will always be there no matter how long it takes to become good enough to become the best.

How about building boats or canoes? Or thinking up a brand new idea. What I am saying is that it is a crime to waste time. Keep saying: 'It is a crime to waste time'. It will eventually dawn on you that it really is. If you want fame and fortune you have to work at it and work really hard but in the end you will have the satisfaction of knowing that you got there by yourself – or, yes, maybe, with just a little help. There are always people around who are willing to help an enthusiastic entrepreneur!

Why not become a dress designer, a dressmaker, a candlestick maker? Why not design teapots that don't drip – there aren't many of those about – or gardens for the elderly? Even if they only have a tiny patch, you will give them such joy. I could go on and on showing you what a crime it is to waste time. Start today! Don't leave it till tomorrow!

England used to be a country of craftsmen respected by all. What wonderful people they were! I remember being fascinated while on holiday watching the local blacksmith at work. These ideas are not only for young people but for all those with time on their hands. You could also become an expert on the environment. Let's face it, you can become whatever you wish to become but – just one word of warning – don't join an overcrowded profession. Choose a job where you can really be the star and you and nobody else can mould your development. Have a go! Like right now!

I am not writing a chapter on negativity because we all have so much of it. We don't need any encouragement to go under when things are bad. It's an entirely natural reaction and in fact we need those negative times in order to maintain a balance.

The trouble is, negativity is difficult to reverse. But

once we feel our verve and electricity returning, it is like a drug; we want more and more of it, and so the mind energy continues to expand and revive.

As I said at the beginning of this book, if you want to keep healthy, try to think positively at all times. No-one in the world can achieve this but if you think you can, you will probably be positive 50 per cent of the time. That is not at all bad – though it would be nice, but difficult of course, if we could achieve a ratio of 70 per cent positive, 30 per cent negative. At the moment there are so many people who exhibit this ratio in reverse!

It is balancing the negative and positive so that you are on an even keel that is difficult, but once you begin to study the process and make it work it is fascinating, absorbing and beautiful. There will be a feeling of fulfilment never before experienced. So, to recap, how do you set about achieving this positivity?

The first step is to limit yourself to five minutes negative thought at a time – then switch off. This is extremely difficult but something you have to do, for unless you do it your thought processes will control you, and not the other way round. With a disciplined mind, *you* are in control.

If you are indoors, look out of the windows and interest yourself in what is going on outside. Is it sunny, rainy, windy? Are there clouds of different shapes? If so, put a face and body to each one. I would be surprised if, with all the shapes you are able to think up, you aren't soon starting to laugh.

And laughter, as I have said, is the beginning of all healing.

If you are outside, look at the people, their expressions, their clothes. I guarantee you will find someone who looks even more miserable than you feel!

At all times tell yourself how lucky you are to have a roof over your head, a bed to sleep in, and food to eat. If you are so unfortunate as to lack one or all of these things, then make up your mind that from now on you will both seek help and help yourself. The point I am making is that you have to put the brakes on and halt negativity at all costs.

Another wonderful way to help yourself is to write everything down. Get a pen and paper and write down everything that comes into your mind – the hate, the guilt, the feelings of rejection, everything. When you have been writing for an hour, take a match and burn the sheet of paper in a ceremonial tin. First of all this will have the effect of dragging everything harmful from the inside to the outside, thus relieving tension.

Secondly, it reduces all the harmful thoughts to ashes. When you have done this several times, you will feel a great sense of relief. But do put the tin in the sink in case of fire!

Even if you are positive it still helps to write things down – but in this case all the *positive* actions you are going to take, and tick them off as you carry them out. Don't reduce them to ashes, however. There is no need.

If you cannot solve your problems at once then you must train yourself to forget them. Negativity is inaction and dangerous. Positivity is action and healthy. Maybe, at first, you will find yourself having as many as twenty five-minute periods of negative thought each day. That doesn't matter, so long as their duration is strictly limited. Eventually you will find that the switching off will be automatic, and little by little the periods themselves will decrease.

Of course we need balance. How else would we know how great it feels to be positive if we were never negative? But if you want a final thought to carry away at the end of this chapter, consider this.

An optimistic, positive person is one who always feels in control. A pessimistic, negative person has the sensation of being washed to and fro by the tide, out of control and unable to gain firm moorings.

An optimist's glass is always half-full.

A pessimist's glass is always half-empty!

Now I will show you three representative characters facing the hazards and challenges of life today, and how they should overcome them.

Twelve

BURN OUT, FADE OUT, WORN OUT

My candle burns at both ends;
It will not last the night;
But oh, my foes, and oh, my friends –
It gives a lovely light.

Edna St Vincent Millay (1892–1950)

So far I have explained how you can expand your mind energy and rid yourself of congestive negative energy which causes compression on every major organ, tissue, and cell; how you can prevent depression by lifting the mind energy off the brain; and how you can link up with cosmic energy by revitalizing not only mind energy but the energy counterpart so that the chakras (energy vortices) are spinning away like Catherine wheels, drawing in more and more life force for the meridian lines to conduct around the body.

What happens if one is unaware of how the energy and physical bodies work together? Or, indeed, if one does not care a rap whether they work together or not? (About 90 per cent of the population probably fall into this category!) To help you sort out these problems, let me present you with a fictional character whom I shall call Andrew.

ANDREW (BURN OUT)

Andrew is one of those men who keep the wheels of business turning. He is extremely ambitious – that is the key to him. He has worked hard all his life and is not afraid of overtime or of taking responsibility. He has a wife, three children and a house for them all to live in which has cost him a pretty penny. You might say he has 'arrived'. Where does he go from there?

The crunch comes when he reaches his early forties and it suddenly dawns on him that he has got to maintain these standards for *the rest of his life*. His wife expects it. His children expect it. As time goes on he begins to feel that he is trapped.

At work younger men are bouncing around the boss, showing how brilliant they are (they haven't got to the wife, house and children stage yet). Andrew knows he is dispensable – everyone is. At night there are things that need doing around the house, but music is blaring in every corner. Andrew's wife would like him to talk to her, and who could blame her, having coped with the children's problems all day as well as the hundred and one other things mums are expected to do.

But Andrew feels tired. Work isn't going as well as it used to. Hundreds more rats have joined the rat race in his firm. Having once been a model husband and father he now shouts at the kids, is unpleasant to his wife, and wants nothing more than to escape for a quiet drink somewhere, probably at his nearest pub.

Andrew is a perfectly normal and average man. His family will recognize him in the brief pen-portrait I have sketched of him and thousands of other Andrews all over the country will identify with him too. What has been happening all these years to make him feel so low mentally and physically now?

The young race around using up energy at a great rate. Almost all of us have done so. Our energy vortices spin cheerfully because life is fun, we are keen to prove ourselves in all manner of different ways, and our mind energy is expanding like crazy because of our positivity. We are drawing in life force faster than we are using it up and the result is an incredible vitality and excess of energy.

Then comes the sobering-up process: the job; the responsibility; the need to get on with people who irritate us, even with people we hate. Andrew finds this too. The boss begins pushing him harder than he would like but ambition still drives him and soon he is promoted – or headhunted, perhaps. At all events he moves on to more and more 'important' positions with more and more people working under him. He becomes responsible for their heartaches, miseries and financial problems as well as his own.

Not surprisingly Andrew has little by little ceased to be the energetic, positive, optimistic person he once was. Negativity has crept in. His mind energy, formerly so expansive, has begun to diminish and funnel inwards, setting up pressure on the brain and tissues which give him intermittent headaches. He has many worries, both at work and at home, yet still he must pretend that he is as vital as he was at twenty.

Alas, negativity can creep up on us all until it becomes our constant companion. With our vortices at half-speed, our bodies compressed by negative energy, and our meridian lines partially blocked we are beginning to feel that old enemy, fatigue. Andrew feels it. Over the years he has been using up more life force than he has been taking in and this is burn out. It can be minor or major but it must be stopped at all costs. There is no way that anyone can continue to achieve with vortices that are half-closed.

What is the answer? First of all, think ahead, give yourself some clairvoyance which, in fact, simply means clear vision. Do you really want so much from life? Would it not be better to have a smaller house and more frequent breaks? Do you really want to be in a position where you are bogged down with other people's problems all the time and so have little time for your partner and children? After all, why does one marry in the first place? To be with the person one loves. Why does one have children? To be with them and play with them; to guide them when needed.

What I am saying is, always leave a good margin of time for yourself when planning a career.

If you are already in Andrew's position then you must give yourself time to practise the exercises in this book. If necessary, have half a day in bed at the weekend reading books on positive thought and vitamin and mineral therapy. You only need to give up half an hour a week to thinking about these things, for them to make a tremendous difference. By thinking positively you are thinking outwards, taking the pressure off the body and allowing the energy vortices to spin again. Stop worrying about your problems. Instead, do something about them by positive thought and you will begin to draw in life force in excess. Believe me, it works!

Whatever you own, whatever your achievements, for the sake of your health be prepared to give them up. Lower your material standards.

Negativity is a killer. You cannot afford it as a constant companion. If you find it difficult to change, try to discipline your thought. Do not allow yourself more than five minutes of negative thinking at any one time. Think outwards, reversing the mind energy so that it expands, linking up to cosmic energy that will aid and support you in your efforts.

Ambition when taken to extremes is a killer. Nobody can afford it. If it doesn't catch up with you when you are young, then it certainly will as you get older. Yes! It's nice to have a beautiful house and an expensive car but so many homes are not real homes, they are merely showplaces, and the people living in them are robots showing off their wares. I have found more love and compassion in homes where the occupants have been satisfied with a lower standard of living so that time – that most precious of all commodities – could be given to a partner or family.

Moving into a smaller house and changing to a smaller car is the most important thing, for with fewer worries, smaller bills, you'll be surprised at the happiness the little things in life bring, things you have forgotten on the way up — to where?

IAN (FADE OUT)

Now let me introduce you to another fictional character. Ian is much younger than Andrew, and much less motivated. He has passed his exams at college but has been unable to find a job that suits him. For two years he has been getting up late, sitting around the house, watching television and listening to the radio, meeting his friends for a drink in the evening, and lounging about with them until late at night. In fact, he has been doing nothing. Not surprisingly, he has become despondent and feels under par all the time.

Why? After all, he has had all the rest he needs and no real money worries as he lives with his parents!

The answer is that with no mind stimulation and very little exercise his mind energy has begun to funnel in, depressing his brain. His energy vortices have slowed down because he hasn't bothered to keep fit or take any exercise. So, in addition, his meridian lines have slowly blocked because they have little energy to conduct around the body.

Ian's whole body is suffering because it is being starved of life force, and something drastic must be done to reverse this process. Ian has got to find the *energy* to re-think his life. This is not going to be easy. Because he is fading out and has a feeling of complete exhaustion, an awful lot of encouragement from friends and family is going to be needed and his own efforts will be needed too, before he can get going again. Once more the old enemy, fatigue, has taken over.

The first thing Ian has got to do is to put on some stout walking boots and start walking, preferably in the country, or, if he's a townsman, through the parks. It would help enormously if a friend, perhaps another young boy or girl in the same state, could accompany him. Together they will stimulate their vortices and by so doing start drawing in more life force by deep breathing. Their tensed muscles will relax also. Their minds will expand, looking toward the horizon or perhaps merely noting the different things they see as they pass – the landscapes, the trees, the hedges, the flowers, even the houses along the roads.

What Ian and his companion will not be doing is thinking about themselves! When you are walking, you must concentrate on becoming more aware of your immediate surroundings and so forget about your own affairs.

If Ian can jump this first hurdle of lethargy – and remember, it really is formidable – then he will feel sufficiently stimulated to attempt the next stage. This is to sit down at home and write on a piece of paper all the things he would like to do but would not have the time to do if he had a job.

This is an extremely interesting exercise and once it has been carried out Ian must look at the situation in reverse and make up his mind to do at least two of these things a week. He must also constantly remind himself that when he has a job he will no longer be able to do them.

The next step Ian will have to take is to make up his mind to improve his talents by learning a skill. Remember, the more talents you have the wider your horizons. Languages are extremely helpful and once you have learned one foreign language it becomes progressively easier to learn more. In addition, a knowledge of languages enables you to find work all over the world, not in English-speaking countries only.

If Ian can achieve these things he will not only be healthy, drawing in life force in excess, but happier and more positive, encouraged by the knowledge that he is no longer wasting his time. Now is the moment when doors will start opening for him. What employers are looking for are energetic young men and women, especially if they are positive and have ways of revitalizing themselves. If you recognize your own situation in the portrait I have drawn of Ian, whether you are a boy or a girl, have a go, snap out of it. You will find it really works!

AUDREY (WORN OUT)

My third fictional character is a young woman, whom I will call Audrey. Here we have the case of an enthusiastic, energetic girl who meets and marries her husband while still pretty young – let us say at the age of nineteen. Almost immediately she has a child, a baby boy, who demands her attention night and day. He is a difficult child, as also is her daughter, born eighteen months later with unfortunate digestive problems.

By now this energetic young woman is beginning to feel the strain. Her husband, also young, is starting out as an electrician, but his experience is small and so is the pay he brings home. In consequence Audrey has to keep on with her part-time job in the evenings as a waitress in a busy restaurant. Although the job is tiring, it gets her out of their tiny flat, enables her to mix with different people, and to this extent is therapeutic.

However, both Audrey and her husband are using more energy than they are drawing in, so the same old reactions that we have met with before set in – vortices slowing down and meridian lines blocking.

Because her first baby was such a bad sleeper, Audrey has grown accustomed to constantly getting up at night. Time and time again her own sleep has been interrupted. Now, mind energy partially leaves us when we sleep in order to rejuvenate us by linking up with cosmic forces. But if brought back with a jolt or a sudden or untimely awakening it gives the physical body a shock which can close the energy vortices. And when this closure in turn causes a diminution of life force, then the meridian lines which conduct the energy round the body start to close up too – there is simply not enough force to keep them open. The result is fatigue. The birth of another baby is a further shock to the system and worry and overwork add more and more to the strain. Obviously, Audrey does manage to re-open the vortices and meridian lines when she plays with the children or takes them out for their walks – she, as well as they, get some exercise on these occasions – and by thinking outwards towards her husband and children she keeps her mind energy expanding. But it is a fight. A few hours of negativity could, once again, bring on fatigue.

Audrey is worn out because her energies are being sapped by her family. What can she do about it? When you have a difficult baby and sleepless nights you have to sleep when the baby sleeps. Never mind the housework – fit that in when you have time. Also see that you always have some frozen food and vegetables in the freezer so that the shopping can be kept to a minimum and skipped entirely on the bad days. If the baby constantly cries during the day, put him in the pram and take him for a walk. That way he can scream and at the same time fill his lungs with fresh air. Audrey will be getting her fill of fresh air too, while the exercise will dislodge some of the negative energy within her body.

If it's pouring with rain and thus impossible to get out, what should Audrey do then? She should run a bath of warm water, get into it with the baby, and swish the water all over its body while relaxing pleasantly herself.

The great rule is not to worry about the little things. Just keep yourself calm and healthy and restore peace to the baby's spirit. After all, being born is in itself extremely traumatic and many babies suffer shock for quite a while afterwards. Few people understand this.

What happens when the second baby arrives? Follow the same instructions. Be positive above all. Whatever is wrong with the baby make up your mind that you will find a way of alleviating the condition, by consulting your GP, studying books on natural alternative methods, and any other means you can.

As your babies start to grow, and from the very first moment when they begin to understand, teach them self-responsibility. For instance, if you tell a child not to do something and it does it, you must make it understand, quite clearly, that it will have to forfeit something it likes. It could be a favourite television programme, sweets, a toy that can't be played with for a few days, or an outing. Let the child choose its own punishment. If it resists then choose it yourself, but give your child the choice in the first place. Obviously no child is going to choose to go without its real favourites, but that doesn't matter.

This is the beginning of the process of making children responsible for themselves and not allowing them to make *you* into an ogre all the time – which is what most of them succeed in doing! They love it when they think they have made you thoroughly ashamed of yourself for being horrid. Don't fall for it! If they insist on doing something horrible like walking into every muddy pool they can find whilst you're out, give them a warning. Say they will have to clean their shoes and wash their own socks if they insist on doing it. Make sure you carry out this warning so that the responsibility lies with them. Of course you won't win. Mums never do, but if you don't introduce self-responsibility when they are young, children will never feel responsible, and as they get older will try passing the buck. I have seen so many people go through their whole lives passing on the responsibility for their actions to someone else. It makes them into really horrible people who have few if any genuine friends.

It really is rather funny when children get used to this kind of discipline, they actually enjoy choosing their own punishment and being responsible. It makes them feel grown up.

Don't give up. Also see that you give your baby healing by placing your hands on it and asking for help. Mother love is the most powerful energy and will automatically enable the mother to heal her child. Always look outwards. Seek knowledge all the time. If possible find a babysitter who will come in once or twice a week while you yourself get right out of the house. All right, perhaps the babysitter will be your husband! If he is no good with babies ask Mum or a friend you can trust, but do it. It will be worth all the effort.

Above all, remember that circumstances can change overnight. Nothing is for ever! Your health and that of your family must always come first. Material things can be acquired little by little and the first things that should be bought should be labour-saving devices and above all a fridge so that food is not wasted. Seek knowledge, buy as many books as you can afford (and don't forget the second-hand shelves, as well as the paperback shelves, for cheap bargains), teach yourself about mineral and vitamin therapy and about herbs that can be used in recipes. Find out about the wonderful natural remedies that are around.

The years when children are small is a fantastic time for parents to educate themselves and reshape their lives. Do it now. Don't wait for tomorrow. The rewards are great and it's you alone who can gather them in!

So what can you learn from the stories of Andrew, Ian and Audrey – examples, respectively, of Burn Out, Fade Out and Worn Out? To put the matter simply, the pace of life nowadays is such that we burn up our energy faster than we draw it in. One of the principal ways of dealing with this is by practising positivity, which expands the mind, linking it up to cosmic energy. When this happens, the energy counterpart stands out from the body about an inch, indicating health. The vortices or chakras are spinning freely.

Negativity inhibits the vortices, slowing them down. Although they are still drawing in energy they are not being supported by the energy counterpart, which has now retracted into the body so that the aura is hardly visible, because the energy is being used up faster than it can be drawn in. The vortices are not rotating fast enough, in fact they are clogging up; and the mind energy, through physical fatigue, has lost its verve and is gradually sinking.

At this stage both the mind and the body need complete rest while they build up their reserves again. And here we come back to the most important part of all – the Mind. It is only when you begin to think sensibly and positively that you realize what you have to do to regain your health.

The same thing happens when we have a virus. We are being attacked and the effort of the counter-attack takes a lot out of our energy system, so that the vortices slow down. But the mind is still active: that is why we can read, write and have telephone conversations even though the body is weak.

A young businessman came to see me a few years ago for healing. He could hardly walk the few feet to my healing room. When I listened to his story it was the same problem I had heard so many times before.

Being ambitious he had worked extremely hard and had achieved a position within his firm which enabled him to have all the luxuries in life. He worked hard and played hard. No harm in that, but what he hadn't taken into account was his particular make-up. Disciplining the mind is the only way we can overcome burn out. This young businessman should have concentrated on his job and rationed his nightlife, eaten sensibly and relaxed as much as possible. Even short, ten-minute relaxation periods can prevent burn-out.

Some people can work physically until they drop but such work is seldom fatiguing to the mind. If you are physically active the negative energies dislodge themselves and the mind energy is released and expands without any particular thought process being involved. However, when your mind is working at full stretch *and* you are overdoing it physically, staying out late at night, drinking too much and eating the wrong foods, then can you wonder if you are in trouble?

We have only so much energy coming in to our support. With a positive attitude to life this intake can be increased. But when energy is used up faster than it is taken in, there can only be one conclusion – a deficit. That is why learning about mind energy and the energy counterpart is so important. Armed with that knowledge you will become highly adept at rationing the energy output when that becomes necessary, which, for all of us, it sometimes will.

If all else fails reduce your income and living standards until you find you can cope with life better. Maybe, after experiencing a worry-free life and the health it brings, you will never want to return to a stressful existence.

You are in control of your mind – have the courage to alter course.

Thirteen

ONE WORLD, ONE HOPE

I have walked a million miles
and seen a million things
that have disturbed my inner being.

The ecology of the Earth disrupted –
a vicious circle of stupidities
and man's inhumanity to man.

All natural instinct crushed
by an *en masse* education,
the tenderness of youth
destroyed by facts and figures.

Where pernicious influences
of the outside world had
not yet reached, only there
did I find peace.

And when the Earth has finally
turned to dust will we
realize, that we have killed
the only source from which we feed.

Betty Shine

You may wonder why I am including a chapter on
the environment, especially as the news is so gloomy.
Every day in our newspapers, and on television and
radio, we hear more and more stories of time

catching up with us. Before I explain my reasons, just consider the following facts.

THE OCEANS

When my children were small we enjoyed camping holidays both in this country and abroad. The Mediterranean was a turquoise joy — warm, sensuous and clear, or so we thought, until we saw raw sewage running over the beaches in Spain. The sight of this ruined many holidays. It was obvious that if nothing was done about it conditions would get even worse.

Now the Mediterranean has become a cesspool. Factories pour their waste into it. Carpets of red algae, the produce of sewage, fertilizer and effluent from cows, pigs and industrial waste, are, at times, visible along certain parts of the coast, while the dead fish and molluscs, starved by these algae of oxygen, are washed up onto the shore. In 1987 a French scientist described this former dream of poets and painters as 'one immense broth of bacteria'.

Elsewhere, things are just as bad, if not worse. Some months ago the London *Sunday Times* published an excellent report from The Hague, where the eight European environment ministers were meeting to discuss North Sea pollution while waste from the lavatories in their own smart congress hall poured incessantly into it. Two months later the *Mail on Sunday* rightly castigated the giant ICI for tipping explosives into the Firth of Clyde. The dumping of chemicals in the seas around Britain has been going on for decades. But of course, few people have wanted to know.

MOTORWAYS

At the time of writing huge chunks are being bulldozed out of the South Downs near my home, leaving ugly scars on the landscape and spoiling once beautiful views. A great deal of Britain, and of other countries too, is being buried under billions of tons of concrete.

NUCLEAR POWER STATIONS

More adults and children living near nuclear power stations suffer from cancer in various forms than those living elsewhere. That cancer and power stations are somehow connected has been obvious for years. Yet the Government are still stonewalling by ordering 'surveys'. This process will go on and on and more and more people will die.

LANDFILL SITES

These are almost as noxious as nuclear power stations. It is appalling that those we elect to represent us have so little care for our welfare. There are hundreds of dangerous chemicals seeping out from sites all over the country. Worst of all nobody knows where three-quarters of them are situated. Big money is involved and, again, nobody cares.

POWER LINES

Overhead cables have been affecting people's health for many years. Andrew Purvis, a Health Correspondent for *Environment Now*, says that in the mid-1960s a study was conducted in Germany to test the effects of electro-magnetic fields on bees. When exposed to extremely low frequency (ELF) signals, the insects sealed up their hives in mid-season and stopped producing honey. In effect, they committed social suicide.

In the mid-1980s experiments showed that ELF signals from overhead cables disorientated birds. After protests from pigeon breeders and bird sanctuaries, high voltage (HV) cables in Gloucestershire were buried underground.

In their recent book *Electromagnetic Man* Cyril Smith and Simon Best examine the possible health hazard of the electrical environment. It is HV power lines that worry them most.

PACKAGING

Plastic is not only horrible to look at but you can't get rid of it. The whole world is turning into a plastic dumping ground. Even if you bury it under the ground it won't rot. Nor can it be re-cycled in any way. Are we then stuck with it? Unless we stop using it, it looks uncomfortably as though we are.

WATER

There is so much effluent discharged into our rivers that it is obvious to everyone that the contamination of our drinking water is not an accident but is deliberately brought about. Money and greed are once more at the root of this evil.

THE OZONE LAYER

First we had the hole in the ozone layer above the Antarctic. Now we have another above the Arctic. The cause is the widespread use of chlorofluoromethane gases, widely used in aerosol sprays, atmospheric testing of nuclear weapons, and the vapour trails of supersonic aircraft.

THE GREENHOUSE EFFECT

This comes about because of excessive heating of the earth's surface through carbon dioxide pollution. Fossil fuels in particular are the baddies in this case. If the demand for more and more energy continues there is no doubt that the Earth will become warmer and climatic changes will occur all over the globe.

RAIN FORESTS

All over the world rain forests are being destroyed. Deforestation means more than just cutting down trees. It means that the essence or aura of the trees is lost and the energy force of the region is gone forever. Natives of affected regions will lose their vital force and be more vulnerable to illness. Living within the aura of the trees gave these people a natural network of healing that has sustained them for centuries. If the nature of energy was even remotely understood in the West this mad policy would never have been countenanced, because the very people who are destroying the trees are also destroying themselves.

CRUELTY TO ANIMALS

Since the beginning of time man has abused animals, and we are no further along the path of improvement. Cruelty to animals all over the world is appalling and unforgivable. It would be impossible in a short space to summarize even a fraction of the atrocities perpetrated every day, many of which take place in our own back yard. In our country of so-called animal lovers cruelty to animals, both farm and domesticated, is getting worse.

Every day the consequences of this inhuman behaviour are coming to light. We are being attacked by a host of bacteria because of the filth that we feed back to our livestock – once more bearing out the law I have so often repeated in this book, that what we give out returns to us tenfold or more.

Now for my reasons for giving you this chapter. First, there is the fact that anger in a good cause can be positive, not negative, and I and many others feel deeply angry about the evils I have just described. We feel frightened, too, because of the consequences that will flow from them; and although fear is generally a negative feeling it becomes positive if it spurs one into action, however late. For over forty years I used to talk to anyone who would listen to me about the terrible things we were doing to our planet. Almost nobody wanted to know and, for me and others like me, those were the really gloomy times. Now at last the message is penetrating. People are doing the double-take – and, moreover, they are getting good leadership. David Icke's book, *It Doesn't Have To Be Like This*, sets out the arguments for Green politics with brilliant cogency. Anita Roddick, with her Body Shops, has vindicated the belief of hundreds of women campaigners – that the practice of testing cosmetics on animals is unnecessary and could be stopped.

So that is my second reason for including this chapter. It is a positive chapter after all. Of course, the battle has hardly begun, and some ominous signs are to be noted. The EEC has some retrograde legislation up its sleeve under which the testing of cosmetics on animals would become compulsory in Britain. Further legislation would abolish the safeguards imposed at present on the export of horses, so dooming them to a terrible fate. But there are positive developments too and here are a handful of them:

People are now fighting for the right to have homes that are not encircled by motorways.

They are insisting that landfill sites shall be registered and that we know what exactly is being put into them.

Power lines are going underground in a lot of places and the Electricity Board are carrying out their own experiments.

Studies are being made of the effect of nuclear power stations. At least that is a start.

Less fossil fuels are being used by big business. People are refusing to use plastic cutlery and many other throw-away items.

The Europeans are insisting that Britain should clean up its water supply.

People are demanding that ivory should be banned to save the few elephants that are left in the world.

The majority of people have now stopped using aerosol sprays that contain CFCs and the suppliers are manufacturing sprays that do not put the environment at risk.

A massive venture has begun to teach the people who are cutting the rain forests that there could be even more wealth in extracting essences for cosmetics and medicines and that this could be a lifetime's supply of wealth, whereas once the trees have gone, that really will be the end.

So what can *you* do? First of all, you can apply pressure — non-violent pressure, that is. Violence is unacceptable. Two wrongs don't make a right. In this respect certain animal rights groups, environmental campaigners and peace protesters are positively counter-productive. But if every woman in the world refused to use cosmetics that have been animal tested, the leading cosmetic firms and the EEC Commission would soon change their minds. If really large numbers of people started writing to their MPs on some environmental issue on which they were all agreed, the MPs would soon take note.

But in fact, if you really want to do your bit to change the world, start with your neighbours. So many lives are made miserable because of neighbourly disputes. Why not be the first to patch up the quarrel and become friends? If the situation between you and your neighbour is very bad, you will at least be doing something if you try not to make it worse. That probably won't be easy but then life isn't easy. If it was, and if we were happy and healthy all the time, then I would not be writing this book! So why not give your neighbour's well-being a little thought? The nearer home you start, the better.

If you would like to live in a clean environment, then start by picking up all the rubbish around your house. No, perhaps you yourself didn't drop it there in the first place, but we have to start somewhere. Just imagine, if we all made sure that our own patch was squeaky clean, how wonderful it would be! It would also make us more determined to speak to anyone we saw dropping litter around, and politely suggest that this wasn't a good idea. We would also put pressure on our local councils to install more waste bins. There are so few around in towns and villages that their littered state is hardly surprising.

We can only change the world little by little. Gradually that little becomes a whole and you will be a part of that wholeness. Your children and their children will eventually have a planet to be proud of and the ability to look at it from afar, way out in the universe. For make no mistake, we are going to have to become travellers in time if we and our world are to survive.

By following the philosophy and exercises in this book you will, without any shadow of doubt, have become more sensitive, more aware. In turn, you will not allow this earth to become a dustbowl for future generations. You will want to know what is happening, not only in this country, but all over the world.

It would be no use your mastering all the techniques in this book, expanding your mind energy and increasing your sensitivity, if the earth you are living in was itself doomed to die. That is the third reason for the inclusion of this chapter. Similarly you yourself must attend to your body's own needs even if your ultimate aim is to go beyond it. This section will therefore end with a discussion of a subject in which common-sense medicine and clairvoyant diagnosis meet – the safeguarding of your health by means of vitamins and minerals.

Fourteen

VITAMIN, MINERAL AND OTHER THERAPIES

Confront disease at its onset.

Persius (AD 34—62)

Not long ago I found myself involved in an argument with a young woman who told me that vitamins were 'all rubbish'. I enquired her age, took a look at the lines on her face, and told her that within the next ten years she would have living and personal proof that she was wrong!

Cosmetic benefits apart, on at least two occasions vitamins have saved my life. The last was when I was living in Spain, some twenty years ago now, and had to have a tetanus injection after an accident. Unfortunately my local doctor, to whom I went for this injection, was no advertisement for medical hygiene. His fingers were dirty and he had just stubbed out a cigarette. The result of his attentions was that I contracted a kidney disease and became so ill that the doctor almost washed his hands of me. 'What are you doing here?' he cheerfully remarked to me later. 'I thought you were dead.'

I was put on penicillin, as much as I was capable of absorbing, thanks to which the main symptoms of the disease cleared up in about three months. But I was left with lesions that could easily tear open. If they did, the disease would restart and my life would once again be at risk.

The danger, I was warned, would be greatest every autumn and spring because of the change in temperature. So, knowing that vitamin E is an emulsifier for scar tissue, both external and internal, I put myself on a massive dose of it, even flying back to Britain to collect my supplies.

I felt so ill I took a very large dose every day. It was a real kill or cure. I wouldn't recommend anyone else to take large doses. That was really my decision. About 1,000 units a day is the most that one should normally take. People with high blood pressure should start on 100 units and lead up to 400 units a day. At all events, after about three weeks I began to feel much better and I have never had the illness back.

There was also the time when I had my daughter Janet and nearly died through haemorrhages. Again I put myself on maxi doses of vitamins and minerals – in particular B Complex which contains B12 – and I believe they saved my life. At any rate, as soon as I started taking them in these large quantities I began to pick up and ever since then, if ever I have been seriously ill, I have done the same thing. The difference is amazing, even after three days.

Vitamins and mineral tablets can be astonishing in their effects – just how astonishing, the following letter shows. But note, as you read it, one other important fact. The young lady who was cured had one vital, built-in advantage – positivity, in the form of determination and an enquiring mind.

That meant that once I had set her on the right track, her own mind energy could do the rest. The story, as written by herself, is as follows:

I work at the firm that publishes Betty's books. As soon as I heard that she would be attending our Autumn Sales Conference in October, 1988, I hoped that I would get a chance to talk to her.

I had been ill for some time. In the summer of 1986, I was told that I had Crohn's Disease, an affliction of the lower intestine which causes abdominal pain. I had taken steroids, spent a month in bed, and was having to be extremely careful about what I ate. I had to avoid dairy produce, chocolate, any fatty food, some meats, avocados and coffee, as they all led to severe pain.

I was also having to be careful about what I *did*. As soon as I got even slightly over-tired, or angry, or tense, the pain would come back and I would have to rest again (rest was the only way to alleviate the symptoms).

Life was becoming restrictive, and rather depressing. I had been told that the disease was chronic, meaning that it could last for years, and that there was no known cause, and no certain cure. So the thought of meeting Betty, and of her being able to give me advice was wonderful.

Betty's presentation to the conference concerned, among other things, the powers of positive thinking and mind energy. She spoke about the Universal Mind. I was attending the conference with Mark, my husband and colleague. We also write fantasy novels together, and we were absolutely amazed to find aspects of Betty's talk coinciding with various ideas that we were currently writing about. We both felt at that point that if we couldn't get to talk to Betty, we'd explode.

We were able to ask for an introduction after dinner. It was an evening I will always remember. We talked with Betty about the Universal Mind, mind energy, the power of positive thinking, and clairvoyance. I asked Betty whether her book would provide its readers with advice on how to cope with an illness.

She immediately told me that I was suffering from an enzyme deficiency that meant my body was unable to digest protein properly. She was able to tell this just by looking at me, and by touching my arm – and without my having given her any indication as to what my problem was. Mark and I were absolutely staggered. Betty then went on to tell me that I should take Papaya enzyme tablets, as they would provide my body with what was lacking. Not only that, but she promptly went off to her bedroom and brought me her own bottle, so that I could start taking the tablets immediately.

At that point, I wanted to go and do handstands on the roof of the hotel! I felt almost transfigured by the most wonderful sense of well-being – and more positive about myself than I had done in a long time. And when Betty rang me a few weeks later to check on my progress, I was able to report that the pain had lessened, and that I felt much better.

That was over two years ago. Since then, I have been able to eat anything I like (because I take the tablets after almost every meal), I feel better now than I have done for ages, have more energy, and have almost forgotten about my 'ailment', which now bothers me only very occasionally.

Betty said to me recently that she felt she had put me

on a different path. She's right — and what a wonderful path it is!

Vitamins are essential restoratives when one is ill. They are no less essential as supplements when one is well. Why is this so? The question is quite reasonable. After all, most people in the West have never had so many foods to choose from as today. Surely our ordinary meals should fulfil our needs. One obvious answer is that most of us don't eat as well as we should.

For one thing, our lives are so rushed. Preparing good meals is time-consuming. If you take the matter seriously and make sure that your food gives you all the vitamins and minerals that you require, you actually have to sit down and work out a whole week's menu. Now that is going to take up a great deal of time – more time than most of us now have. I often don't have time to think about what I am going to eat and I'm sure millions of people are like me in that respect. There are lovely books telling you what a wonderful thing it is to eat beautiful, nutritious salads. Unfortunately most people simply don't have the time to buy them, wash them, shred them, and serve them up. At lunch they are more likely to grab a cheese sandwich, which is high in cholesterol, and a packet of crisps or something like that. In the evening they may let themselves go on a hamburger, which is equally unbalanced fare. So it is not so stupid to start the day by taking the vitamins necessary to set you up.

If you have the time to prepare balanced meals,

wonderful. If you don't, diet as sensibly as you can but as a prevention take your vitamin and mineral tablets first. That is really why I always advocate supplementation. Nowadays busy people just do not have the time even to think about what they should be eating, let alone to get down to preparing it. Another good reason for slowing down and getting out of the rat race!

There is also the fact, which cannot be altered merely by changing to a more sensible life style, that many people cannot absorb into their systems some of the vitamins and minerals in the food they eat. They do not break the food down. An awful lot of food goes through an awful lot of people intact, so that they get no benefit at all from the vitamins and minerals contained in it. That is why vitamin and mineral supplements are necessary – for remember, these supplements are concentrated food, not drugs. Even people who think they have no problems in this respect may be in for a nasty shock, when they discover, perhaps ten or twenty years on, that they have been deficient in some vitamin or mineral all their lives without realizing the fact.

As a child, during the war, I was evacuated to the country where I was underfed, indeed half starved, by the strange couple who took me in. Not surprisingly, as a result, I developed horrendous anaemia. Years later, when I had had my own children, I developed anaemia again and I thought, why is this? I am eating well. I always eat well. So I started buying books on vitamins. The first thing they showed me was that I needed all the B Complex vitamins. Then I came across a book by Barbara Cartland. I found it in my local health store and it proved exceptionally helpful. From it I learned that I was lacking in calcium, so I put myself on bonemeal tablets and the problem I had disappeared. From that day to this I have made a study of vitamins and mineral therapy and know for a fact that I should be less healthy than I am if I had not taken supplementation.

Some time ago I discovered that I could diagnose clairvoyantly what vitamins people need. That is a special gift, but anybody can read books. Sample one or two of them – most of them are quite cheap – and try and discover what you actually need. Too many people charge into health food shops saying can I have vitamin E, can I have ginseng, and so on. They are wasting their money. There is no point in taking supplements for vitamins or minerals in which you are not deficient. To start with, just take a general vitamin and mineral to keep you going. Then read the book. Then return to the shop armed with at least some knowledge. You will drop some vitamins and take up others and eventually you will come out with a nice little list that fits your need because you have experimented. Remember, too, to refine your own instincts and trust them. Listen to your body. It is always sending you messages. For instance, I can sense whenever I am low in potassium, and instinctively take the necessary steps to remedy the deficiency, generally by eating bananas. All healthy people do this without thinking about it, but nowadays instinct and emotions are at a premium — we have to pause in the bustle of our daily lives and consciously retrain.

Of course, not everything you instinctively crave is going to be good for you — far from it, in fact. You have to use your common sense. But behind every craving, however injurious, there is a cause. For instance, a person with a craving for sugar and sweets may be deficient in the vitamins and minerals which cause the craving. Alcoholics are deficient in the whole of the vitamin B spectrum. And so on. Any such addiction is a hope for remedy against depression or deprivation of one sort or the other. Giving in to it brings you a quick high — but an even lower low. The alcoholic becomes even more deficient in vitamin B than he was before. The sweet-eater gets fat, and may even become diabetic. The one good thing that any addiction can produce is an awareness of the fact that we are deficient in some essential. We must then use our intelligence — and, where necessary, our strength of mind — to correct the deficiency in the right way, not the wrong one.

A course of the right vitamins will help you to do this, but take it gently, don't become a fanatic, and remember that supplementation is not just for the short term, it is for life. A two-months' crash course on bananas is unlikely to be the whole answer! But little by little, as your supplementation takes effect, you will start noticing a subtle change.

Never neglect the purely physical sides of your life. They interact constantly with your mental and spiritual sides and their interaction is vital. I have shown in this book how mind energy affects the bodily state. But the bodily state can also expand – or, when it is poor, restrict – the mind energy.

A proper intake of vitamins and minerals is essential to physical health, and a deficiency of them is at the bottom of most health problems. So here is a selective list – I am not trying to compete with the specialist books and manuals – of some of the most important of them and of some of the needs they meet.

VITAMINS

Vitamin A

If your diet contains liver, butter, cheese and eggs you are almost certainly getting enough of this vitamin. A deficiency would cause night-blindness, inflammation of the mucous membranes, and kidney stones, but such a combination is unlikely to be manifested outside countries suffering from famine conditions, where the victims would of course be deficient in every other vitamin too.

Vitamin A contains carotene, so an overdose would be highly toxic, and I never recommend this vitamin by itself. Included in a mineral and vitamin capsule it is, however, perfectly safe. A supplement of halibut liver oil also ensures your daily supply.

Vitamin B

B1. Thiamine: Found in brewer's yeast, brown rice, wholemeal bread and liver.

Deficiency symptoms: fatigue, irritability, bad concentration, muscle weakness and palpitation. If you find yourself getting testy with your nearest and dearest, this may be what you need!

B2. Riboflavin: Found in liver, cheese, pulses, yoghurt, green vegetables, egg white and brewer's yeast.

Deficiency symptoms: dizziness, insomnia, over-sensitivity to light.

B3. Niacin: Best source is brewer's yeast.

Deficiency symptoms: mental problems, depression, anxiety, insomnia, inflammation of the tissues.

B6. Pyridoxine: An anti-depressant vitamin good for combating premenstrual tension and of general benefit for any woman who is taking the Pill.

Found in bananas, brown rice, white fish, brewer's yeast, nuts and dried fruits.

Deficiency symptoms: depression, premenstrual syndrome, asthma.

B12. Cobalamin: Found in fish (of the fatty sort), eggs, chicken, yoghurt and cow's milk.

Deficiency symptoms: pernicious anaemia, irritability and states of nervous collapse.

B15. Bangamic Acid: Safest as a component of a mixed mineral and vitamin tablet, since one of its principal sources is apricot stones, which contain arsenic. Should *always* be on prescription if taken on its own.

No known deficiency symptoms, but many incidental benefits, principally in support of the blood sugar metabolism and liver functions.

Note on the B Vitamins: Except for B6, which is especially efficacious as a cure for stress and premenstrual tension, and B12, which is used to treat serious cases of anaemia and (by injection) shingles, these vitamins are best taken together in a complex tablet, since they work in conjunction with each other. As such, they are particularly to be recommended for all conditions of nerves and stress.

Vitamin C

The wonder vitamin. Effective against almost every affliction known to man, from the common cold to failure of the immune system. I recommend a dose of at least 3 grams a day for everyone, and up to 10 grams a day for cancer patients. It must however be *natural* vitamin C, with bio-flavanoids, as obtainable from good health stores. Ascorbic acid is better for short periods in cases of colds, as it works faster, but not as beneficial in the long term as natural vitamin C. For colds, take 2 grams four times a day until better; for influenza 2 grams five times a day. I myself take 6 to 8 grams a day.

This vitamin is an anti-oxidant, thus it counteracts cell oxidation, a cause of sickness and rapid ageing. Its other deficiency symptoms include irritability, joint pains, small and large haemorrhages, bleeding of the gums, and sore mouth.

Among its principal food sources are rosehip syrup, acerola cherry, blackcurrants, lemon juice, orange juice, bananas, fresh fruit in general, parsley, white cabbage – but the list is endless.

Note that orange juice should be freshly squeezed. A carton of orange juice has only to be open to the air for a very short time for its vitamin content to be seriously reduced. And unfortunately an orange that hasn't ripened on the tree – that is, probably every orange you buy in a shop – is approximately 7 per cent less rich in vitamin content too, as is well known. In fact, it is extremely difficult to know how much vitamin C any food you eat contains. Hence the need to take tablets.

Vitamin D

Found in cod liver oil, sardines, salmon, eggs and dairy products.

Deficiency symptoms: bow legs, muscular weakness leading to spasm, bone pain.

This is the most toxic vitamin of all. Apart from what is ingested with food, take only in cod liver oil capsules or incorporated in vitamin and mineral supplements. Regular sunlight is necessary to avoid vitamin D deficiency in winter. Try to get outdoors as much as possible, even if the sun isn't shining.

Vitamin E

D-alpha Tocopherol (natural); d1-alpha tocopherol (synthetic).

When purchasing, preferably from a good health store, make sure that d-alpha tocopherol, the natural variety, and not d1-alpha, the synthetic variety, is on the label. Found in wheatgerm oil, sunflower oil, soya oil, cod liver oil, potato crisps, peanut butter, brown rice, salmon, apples, bananas and strawberries.

Deficiency symptoms: decreased sexual performance, lethargy, irritability, heart problems.

This vitamin is an anti-oxidant. It is a highly effective anti-thrombin. The doctors Evan and Wilfrid Shute in America have used it for decades and have saved lives with it, especially in heart ailments. It carries oxygen through the body and strengthens the heart muscle.

When taking vitamin E for the first time, start with 100 units a day and work up. As I have already explained, if you suffer from high blood pressure never take more than 400 units a day. I have been taking this vitamin for thirty-two years and I take approximately 900 units a day.

Vitamin E is another wonder vitamin. As an

anti-oxidant it is especially effective, along with vitamin C, in reducing the progress of ageing.

Vitamin K

Found in Brussels sprouts, cauliflower, broccoli, tomatoes, string beans, spinach, beef and pig liver, peas, cow's milk and alfalfa.

Deficiency symptoms: viral hepatitis, cirrhosis, cancer. No need for supplementation beyond that found in the multi-vitamin formula.

Note: A strong vitamin and mineral tablet, taken every day, is absolutely necessary to combat the stress of modern living and the harmful effects of fast and dead foods, too much sugar and fat in diet, alcohol, and smoking.

MINERALS

As essential as vitamins to the healthy functioning of our bodies, and as harmful if we become deficient in them, minerals too often need to be supplemented to restore their full supply. A hair analysis can be carried out nowadays to discover any lack.

The following is a list of the most important of the body's minerals, their principal food sources, the disorders they heal and those that appear when they are absent.

Calcium

The body contains more of this mineral than of any

other. It is essential to the health of our bones, skeletons and teeth. It helps the body to assimilate iron, speeds the recovery of people suffering from operations and infections, and steadies the heart beat. Lack of it causes insomnia and emotional problems.

Vitamin D is essential to the absorption of calcium – always make sure, when buying a calcium supplement, that vitamin D has been added to it. In addition to its presence in multi-vitamin and mineral tablets, it can also be bought in the form of chelated calcium, where amino acids have been used to help absorption into the blood stream. Take calcium tablets for headaches, muscle cramps, nervous tics and other signs of nervous disorder.

Principal food sources: milk and milk products, cheese, sardines, soya beans, peanuts, sunflower seeds, and green vegetables.

Chlorine

This mineral assists in the cleansing of body wastes, but is present in our water supply so that supplements are seldom required.

Best natural food sources: salt, kelp, olives.

Chromium

Vital in maintaining correct blood sugar levels, and thus essential to diabetics. Best taken in vitamin and mineral tablets, especially brewer's yeast tablets or powder. Take a few tablets a day.

Best food sources: kidneys, liver, mushrooms, shellfish and blackstrap molasses.

Cobalt

This mineral, essential for the supply of red blood cells, is present in small quantities in vitamin B12, and if you are getting enough of that vitamin, you are getting enough cobalt. Vegetarians may be deficient in it, so should take a vitamin and mineral tablet that includes vitamin B12.

Best food sources: kidney, liver, meat, milk, oysters and clams.

Copper

Essential for the proper activation of vitamin C. Aids iron absorption. Also activates the amino acid tyrosine, which works as the pigmentation factor on skin and hair. Wearing a copper bracelet enables copper to be absorbed by the skin, and its anti-inflammatory properties benefit sufferers from rheumatism and arthritis. But too much copper lowers the body's zinc levels, causing insomnia, hair loss and depression.

Found in green leafy vegetables, whole grain products, liver. No need for supplementation if you are getting enough of these. It is also present in vitamin and mineral supplementation.

Dolomite

This consists of calcium and magnesium in the proportion of two to one, is the perfect supplement. Other mineral and vitamin supplements also contain it in small amounts.

The enzymes necessary for the body's use of vitamin B1 and vitamin C have need of this mineral to activate them. It is also important in the formation of thyroxine, the principal hormone of the thyroid gland. It eliminates fatigue, and stimulates muscle reflexes and the nervous system.

Some food sources: green, leafy vegetables, peas, beets, egg yolks and whole grain cereals. Found in vitamin and mineral supplements.

Fluorine

Counteracts dental caries but too much of it can discolour the teeth. As a rule additional fluorine will not be required.

Sources: drinking water, seafood and gelatin. Not found in mineral and vitamin supplements.

Iodine

Two thirds of the body's iodine is found in the thyroid gland, which the iodine controls and which in turn controls the metabolism. Iodine deficiency leads to a slow-down in mental activity, a gain in weight, and a loss of energy. It can also cause goitre.

Food sources: kelp, onions and all sea food. Kelp is found in mineral and vitamin supplements. Taken by itself in tablet form it protects the thyroid from the effects of radiation.

Iron

This mineral is necessary for the production of haemoglobin (red blood corpuscles), myoglobin (red pigment in muscles), and certain enzymes. It is one of the two major dietary deficiencies in women, the other being calcium.

Found in liver, heart, red meat, beans, asparagus, molasses, oatmeal, soya beans, yeast extract, almonds. Also included in vitamin and mineral supplements.

Magnesium

This mineral facilitates calcium and vitamin C metabolism and is essential for nerve and muscle function. It is an anti-stress mineral which assists in fighting depression. It also helps to prevent calcium deposits, kidney stones and gallstones. Alcoholics are usually lacking in it.

Food sources include: lemons, figs, almonds, seeds, apples and dark green vegetables.

Molybdenum

Assists in carbohydrate and fat metabolism. Prevents anaemia. There is no need for supplementation.

Found in whole grains, dark green, leafy vegetables.

Phosphorus

Present in every cell in the body. Niacin cannot be assimilated without it, and it is also needed for transference of nerve impulses.

Some food sources: fish, poultry, eggs, seeds, nuts, whole grains and meat. Bonemeal is a natural source of phosphorus.

Potassium

A major factor in the body's water balance. Deficiency results in bad water retention (edema), low blood sugar (hypoglycaemia), and mental and physical stress, which in turn can cause it. Potassium tablets are now available in the form of gluconate, and it is found in vitamin and mineral supplements.

Food sources include: watercress, potatoes, sunflower seeds, mint leaves, bananas and citrus fruits -- so if you sense a deficiency, drink plenty of orange juice as a quick pick-me-up.

Selenium

Selenium, like vitamin E and vitamin C, is an anti-oxidant, and so prevents the hardening of the tissues and other symptoms of premature ageing. It also serves to prevent cancer and heart disease, and low selenium has also been found to be a factor in cot deaths. Men have a greater need of it than women, as half their bodies' supply is in the testicles and portions of the seminal ducts. Selenium is also lost in semen. Selenium has been neutralized by fertilizers and there are few places in Britain where significant amounts of it can now be found in the soil. Therefore one tablet of Selenium ACE every morning before food is a must.

Some food sources (in so far as this mineral is any longer present at all): tomatoes, broccoli, tuna fish, onions, wheat germ.

Silicon

Silicon is very beneficial for people with weak nails.

Food source: unrefined cereals.

Sodium (Salt)

We suffer from too much of it rather than too little, so no need for supplements unless you are in a hot climate as sodium is lost through sweat.

Sulphur

Essential for hair, nails and skin. Maintains oxygen balance. No known deficiency symptoms. Creams and ointments containing it have been used successfully to treat a variety of skin ailments.

Vanadium

Inhibits the formation of cholesterol and helps to prevent heart attacks. No other known deficiency symptoms.

Food source: fish.

Zinc

An essential element in the protection of the immune system, this mineral also accelerates the healing of external and internal wounds, promotes growth and mental awareness, and is a factor in the treatment of schizophrenia, anorexia nervosa and depression. It maintains the body's acid-alkaline balance, and contributes to protein synthesis.

Some food sources: steak, lamb, wheat germ, brewer's yeast, pumpkin seeds, eggs.

Zinc tablets in the form of gluconate can be bought at health food stores. They are sucked and kept in the mouth as long as possible and are extremely effective in easing and curing infections and sore throats. Zinc cold tablets can be bought at ordinary chemists and used in the same way.

Chelated zinc can be taken every day as a protection against illness. Small amounts of the mineral are also present in vitamin and mineral supplements.

OTHER SUBSTANCES

Acidophilus

Source of friendly intestinal bacteria also found in yoghurt. Used in conjunction with antibiotics, it prevents diarrhoea and an overgrowth of Candida Albicans, a type of fungus which is found in the intestines, lungs, vagina and mouth (where it is called thrush), on fingers and under finger nails. Generous doses of acidophilus culture banish these symptoms in only a few days, but less massive amounts should be taken regularly to encourage the growth of healthy bacteria and to keep the intestines clear. Acidophilus reduces gas and swelling of the stomach, assists digestion and gives a feeling of well-being. Combined with pectin in tablet form it is particularly beneficial. It should be used in large amounts for the treatment of Myalgic Encephalomyelitis (ME or 'Yuppie Flu').

It is available from health food stores. I particularly recommend Blakemores' Acidophilus Plus Pectin.

Evening Primrose Oil

Evening Primrose is a weed of the willow herb family with bright yellow flowers on medium stems which open in the evening, hence its name. It has no connection with the more familiar spring flower found in gardens and woods. Evening Primrose Oil is extremely beneficial when taken in the first stages of MS (multiple sclerosis). It also helps sufferers from asthma, eczema and Sjogren's syndrome (when coupled with vitamin B6 and vitamin C). It lowers the cholesterol level and is thus a good dieting aid.

More and more diseases are responding to Evening Primrose Oil therapy. It is available from health food stores.

Ginseng

Concoction produced from a parsnip-like root which the Chinese have used for centuries as an aphrodisiac and all-round pick-me-up. Effective in the treatment of high and low blood pressures, poor circulation, and the side-effects of radiation. Obtainable in tablet form from health food stores and some chemists.

Honey

Absolutely pure honey from a single hive, as obtainable in certain health food shops, not a mixture of honeys from different hives, can work wonders in healing ulcers and burns. Spread on the affected part and bandage up if external. If internal, swallow. Use in conjunction with vitamin C – the healing vitamin.

Kelp

This amazing seaweed contains more vitamins and minerals than any other food. Because of its natural iodine content it has a normalizing effect on the thyroid gland, is a useful aid to dieting, and is particularly effective against flatulence and rheumatism.

Can be bought in tablet form from health food stores.

Lecithin

Every cell in the body contains this substance. A product of the soya bean, it is a biological emulsifier, nature's own pipe cleaner which scours the arteries, protects the heart, and controls the cholesterol level. Supplements either in capsule or granule form should be taken every day. Better still are granules which can be sprinkled over fruit or cereal, or added to protein powder drinks. An invaluable adjunct to the diet.

Papaya

This substance, taken in tablet form, aids the digestion of proteins and is a must for MS sufferers. Take two before each meal.

Propolis

This precious, but little-known substance, a powerful antibiotic, comes from the sticky mess found in the bottom of beehives. The bees land on it before entering, which is why the hives are sterile. I have been using propolis in capsule form, in throat pastilles or in cream, for decades. It is also a tonic. There is no need to take this substance every day. Just keep it in the medicine cupboard for use in tablet form against infectious viruses, flu or colds, as pastilles for throat infections, and in the form of cream for the treatment of wounds. Can be bought at health stores.

Note

I would also recommend to readers of this book a guide called *The Amino Revolution* by Dr Robert Erdmann and Meiron Jones. It is about amino acids, the building blocks of protein, which I have been taking in capsule form for years, and is a lucid treatment of a complicated but important subject. In other ways, too, you must seek knowledge for yourself. Never forget that every attempt to increase awareness expands the MIND ENERGY and benefits the whole of life.

REMEDIES

To conclude this chapter, and make it better for reference, here is a list of some of the problems and ailments to which I have successfully applied vitamin and mineral therapy over the years. Of course, when I am diagnosing patients clairvoyantly and am in touch with them either personally or by letter, I am able to be very specific about exactly what each of them needs, especially as regards minerals and the sub-groups of vitamin B. In a book this is impossible – my advice can only be general. All the more reason then to expand your mind energy and learn to prescribe for yourself!

Study these lists. Become sensitive to your body's needs. If you think you may be deficient in one vitamin or mineral, give it a try – and continue taking it for long enough to give it time to produce an effect. If it does nothing for you and you find you were on the wrong track, then experiment with something else. I believe that all vitamins and minerals interact anyway.

But remember, not every illness is amenable to vitamin and mineral therapy. Therefore, if a health problem fails to respond to this treatment, please seek the advice of your doctor without delay.

With that warning given, here is my selected list.

Acne

I have recommended zinc for the treatment of acne for many years and in 95 per cent of cases it has greatly reduced or cured this condition. I advise 10–15 mg per day until the trouble clears up. Selenium has also helped acne sufferers. One Selenium ACE tablet per day has been found effective not only in clearing the skin but in curing the aches and pains which young people experience during their major 'growing' period. These youngsters should at all costs avoid food containing sugar, which unquestionably has a bad effect on the skin. This advice applies to adults as well!

Alcohol Dependency

B Complex tablets, taken every day, together with a strong vitamin and mineral capsule, help to combat this condition.

Allergies

I usually recommend anti-oxidants for all allergies. These vitamins prevent oxidation of cells which is also an ageing process. I recommend Selenium ACE, plus 2 gram of vitamin C a day.

Alopecia *(hair loss)*

Take a strong multi-vitamin and mineral tablet every day, plus 2 gram of vitamin C and zinc tablets. There will be zinc in the multi-vitamin tablet but take the extra dose as instructed on the container until the hair begins to grow normally again.

Anaemia

Take B Complex with a vitamin and a mineral tablet that contains B12.

Angina

Obviously people with angina will be under medical supervision but I have found that garlic capsules and halibut liver oil capsules plus 2 gram of vitamin C a day can ease the pain associated with this disease. The garlic capsules are best taken at night with cold water. Usually four capsules will be sufficient.

Appetite, Loss of

I have found a multi-vitamin and mineral tablet taken every day with four garlic capsules last thing at night plus zinc tablets helps to restore the appetite to normal if it is only a short-term problem. If it is a long-term problem, seek medical aid. Do not allow this condition to continue.

Arthritis

There are so many types of arthritis that it is impossible to name them all, but there is no doubt that over the years Selenium ACE tablets have proved of tremendous benefit in alleviating the crippling pain of this disease. Take two tablets in the morning before breakfast and after two months reduce this to one tablet a day for the rest of your life. It has been found that people suffering from arthritis, as also from cancer, have little or no selenium in their system. Also take 2 gram of vitamin C a day plus cod liver oil capsules as well as four garlic capsules at night before going to bed. This sounds a lot but is very little compared to all the different foods we handle every day.

Asthma

I usually advise B Complex, 400 units vitamin E. (If you have high blood pressure take 100 units a day to begin with and gradually increase the dose. If you begin to react then go back to the highest dosage with which you found you were comfortable.) I have never known anyone in the sixteen years I have been practising who has suffered any adverse effects from taking vitamin E, plus 2 gram of vitamin C per day, as for allergies, above.

Back Problems

These can be caused by all sorts of troubles, especially kidney diseases. It is advisable to seek medical help. Once you have done so and your particular problem has been identified, then try taking 4 gram of vitamin C a day to help the healing process, plus B Complex, and 800–1500 mg of calcium daily until the pain disappears.

Bed Wetting

This is a very common complaint among children and all sorts of physical and non-physical problems can be the cause. I have found that extra calcium can have a very beneficial effect, so milk drinks and whatever else supplies it, are recommended. Avoid fruit drinks near bed time. Goats' milk or soya milk, if an allergy is involved, also helps the child to relax. If you have the time, story-telling is a wonderful way of relaxing children before sleep and also helps to make them feel secure. Insecurity can be one of the causes of this complaint. Playing their own cassettes, especially book cassettes, can be an excellent idea too.

Bowel Upsets

This ailment can have many causes, but for ordinary

everyday upsets you can do no better than take Acidophilus and Pectin tablets. If you cannot get Pectin, Acidophilus on its own is all right. Tests in America have proved that Acidophilus is well worth carrying around with you on holiday, as it can prevent food poisoning if taken before each meal.

Breasts, Painful or Lumpy

By taking 400 units of vitamin E, Evening Primrose Oil and 2 mg of vitamin C this condition can be cured or greatly alleviated. Again, if you have high blood pressure start with 100 units of vitamin E, gradually increasing to 400 units a day. It would also be beneficial to cut out caffeine, so keep off coffee, chocolate, and so on.

Bronchitis

Take 4 gram of vitamin C a day plus zinc tablets. A course of vitamin and mineral therapy can also help to set you back on your feet.

Burns

Bicarbonate of soda made into a paste and gently applied to the afflicted area of skin prevents blistering and pain. Cold running water also helps to reduce the heat if poured onto the burn straight away. Vinegar is also efficacious, and so is honey. After the worst stages have passed, vitamin C (4 gram a day) and zinc tablets can speed the healing process. Obviously if the burns are major ones, you will have sought medical aid.

Caffeine Dependency

All those who cannot get through the day without numerous cups of coffee are caffeine dependent. The problem with caffeine is that it has some very nasty after-effects such as depression, jumping sensations in the legs, abnormal heart beat, painful breasts and tremor. The depressive aspect is the most common. Try to cut out coffee altogether if you can. Reducing the amount you drink doesn't seem to work — if you are truly an addict you will only want more! Substitute a fruit drink instead, or a nice long cold glass of spring water which will make you feel clean inside. In any event you should take B Complex to help you overcome your addiction, plus 2 gram of vitamin C a day.

Candida Albicans

This problem is so common that nearly everyone I meet nowadays shows some indication of infestation by the fungus which is the villain of the piece here, getting out of hand through too much sugar consumption and too many antibiotics. Symptoms are belching, bloated stomach, palpitations caused by pressure on the heart, aching limbs and joints and a general feeling of being unwell and out of sorts. Cure: chew two Acidophilus and Pectin tablets three times a day.

Coeliac Disease

This is an intolerance to a protein called gluten

which is present in rye, barley, wheat and oats. Obviously these things should be avoided but I have found in many cases that Acidophilus and Pectin tablets between meals and Papaya Enzyme with meals negate the bad effects of these foods. Both Acidophilus and Papaya can be found in your local health store.

Conjunctivitis and Inflamed Eyelids

Take a vitamin B Complex tablet every day. Plus 2 gram of vitamin C. Zinc tablets are also recommended.

Colitis and Colic

As for Crohn's Disease below.

Constipation

Obviously if you have been constipated for a long time you will have seen your doctor about it. But whether the affliction is long or short term you should be eating food with a lot of fibre content such as whole grains, fruit, nuts, seeds and plenty of fresh vegetables. Adding a little bran to your cereal every morning can help also, but don't add too much – a level tablespoon should be sufficient. I also recommend Ortis fruit cubes.

Cramp

Cramp in muscles is very common and has many possible causes, but calcium tablets taken every day may be of help, especially to the over-forties.

As people get older they are unable to absorb calcium from their food as efficiently as they did when young.

Crohn's Disease

People suffering from this disease should try as far as possible to eliminate sugar from their diet, since a high sugar intake appears to be one of its causes, or at least to aggravate it. I recommend two tablets of Papaya Enzyme with meals and two tablets of Acidophilus and Pectin between meals. Both these tablets can be chewed and are pleasant to take.

Dandruff

I have found a multi-vitamin and mineral tablet with Acidophilus and Pectin tablets extremely beneficial for this complaint.

Depression

This dreaded affliction can be brought on by so many causes, mental and physical, that curing it may be difficult. But a vitamin and mineral tablet plus 2 gram vitamin C per day and Amino Acid Complex really can be of help. Please consult your doctor if the depression continues.

Diabetes

Everyone must seek medical treatment for this condition, as soon as it is suspected, but in addition I have found that by recommending vitamin E capsules and 3 gram of vitamin C per day I have enabled my clients' doctors to reduce their insulin intake. Start by taking 100 units and gradually increase to 400 units over six weeks. It is certainly worth a try.

Diarrhoea

Acidophilus and Pectin tablets chewed twice a day may do good. Once more, it depends on the cause.

Digestive Problems

Take two Papaya tablets with meals and two Acidophilus and Pectin tablets between meals.

Early Morning Sickness

This is really miserable, coming just at a time when one ought to be feeling on top of the world. Try having a glass of pure orange juice by the bedside ready to drink in the morning before getting up. Also take a vitamin and mineral tablet each day. Wrist bands, obtainable at chemists and health stores, also help, you may be surprised to hear. They have a little button that presses on an acupuncture point and have been found most beneficial.

Eczema

A vitamin and mineral tablet, Amino Acid Complex, zinc tablets, and Evening Primrose Oil (500 mg to be taken orally), have been found beneficial in counteracting this complaint. Evening Primrose Oil can also be applied to the skin. Children with eczema can be given a vitamin and mineral tablet of suitable strength, and a quarter dose of Evening

Primrose Oil. A relaxation tape can benefit adults and children alike, as this condition can be brought on by stress.

Fainting

Can be due to hypoglycaemia, or low blood sugar. Try drinking 2–3 glasses of fruit juice every day, especially before rising. It can also be due to Candida Albicans, so try also Acidophilus and Pectin tablets. If fainting continues then it is essential to consult your doctor.

Flushing due to Menopause

Vitamin E is a must for all women during the menopause, but especially for those who suffer from hot flushes. Begin with 200 units and gradually increase over a period of two months to 600 units.

Halitosis (Bad Breath)

Poor health causes this, so take a vitamin and mineral tablet, zinc, 2 gram of vitamin C, Amino Acid Complex plus Acidophilus and Pectin tablets. Also four garlic capsules with cold water every night.

Hay Fever

Sufferers from this trying affliction dread the spring, and early summer, and who can blame them? I recommend them to cut sugar out of their diet altogether, and over the years this course has produced dramatic results. Many of my clients have found their hay fever relieved after excluding meat from their diet, so why not experiment with this too? A course of pollen tablets could also be tried.

Headaches

If these are infrequent, try taking calcium tablets: they relax the muscles and thus allow the blood to flow freely. They take longer to work than drugs, though there is no doubt that they are effective. So, after taking them, relax for half an hour.

Hypertension (High Blood Pressure)

Obviously you will seek medical attention for this complaint but I also recommend garlic capsules, to be taken four every evening with a glass of cold water. Taking these regulates the stickiness of the platelets which causes the problem, and they also act as a preventative. Everyone over the age of thirty should take garlic capsules every day. Doing so has enabled many of my clients to take much lower doses of drug or cut them out altogether. You must of course be guided by your doctor on this.

The Immune System

If you find that you are catching more colds, flu or other virus diseases than you should, then please take 3 gram of vitamin C every day with zinc, multi-vitamin and mineral tablet, and Amino Acid Complex.

Influenza

As above, plus plenty of fruit drinks and a light diet. Stay in bed until the fever has disappeared. Also try the time-honoured drink of whisky, honey and lemon – it makes you feel a lot better!

Insomnia

Amino Acid Complex with a vitamin and mineral tablet has been found extremely helpful in alleviating this condition, as has tryptophan (an amino acid) taken on its own before bed. Do not continue to take tryptophan on its own for any length of time. Amino Acid Complex, however, can be taken every day for the rest of your life! The dosage then is two tablets of the Amino Acid Complex to be taken in the morning with the vitamin and mineral tablet, and two before bedtime. These tablets contain tryptophan in smaller amounts.

Legs (Aching)

Many conditions can cause this, but if a blockage in the venous system is the one responsible, then lecithin granules taken every day will act as a pipe cleaner. Lecithin is the only natural substance that emulsifies cholesterol. For other symptoms try Vegetex herbal tablets. I have recommended them to hundreds of my clients with very positive results.

Memory, Loss of

I usually recommend zinc tablets for this, with good results so far.

Multiple Sclerosis

The majority suffering from this condition can be

helped by taking a multi-vitamin tablet, Amino Acid Complex and, to aid digestion, two Papaya tablets with food and two Acidophilus and Pectin tablets between meals.

Pre-Menstrual Tension (PMT)

This has been alleviated by taking B Complex and Evening Primrose Oil capsules a week before each period is due. Also calcium tablets taken every day throughout the month help you to relax. A lot of pre-menstrual tension is due to lack of calcium.

Prostate Problems

Try eating Pumpkin Seeds (you can obtain them from your local health stores). Zinc tablets are also a must with this condition. If problems persist then seek the advice of your doctor.

Psoriasis

This is a very distressing ailment but I have treated it with zinc supplementation and 4 gram of vitamin C a day, with good results.

Rheumatism

A good general herbal tablet like Vegetex helps alkalize the acidity in the system.

Shingles

Another nasty complaint that leaves the sufferer with depression and pain sometimes lasting for years.

Take large doses of vitamin C (about 6 gram a day), zinc tablets and a vitamin and mineral tablet. Also ask your doctor for B12 injections. This can relieve the pain and prevent it returning.

Large doses of vitamin C can cause loose bowels. If this happens, cut back to the amount that suits you.

Sinus Infection

Take 4 gram of vitamin C a day, together with zinc tablets, and use an inhalation of Olbas Oil as well as a little gently rubbed inside the nose at night so that the treatment continues. Olbas Oil rubbed on the forehead and around the cheeks at night relieves the pain. You can also take Olbas Oil pastilles.

Skin Problems

Take zinc tablets plus 3 gram of vitamin C. Propolis cream is also beneficial.

Sore Throats

Take a course of propolis capsules and propolis or Olbas Oil pastilles. Gargling with TCP also brings great relief.

Sores

Try using propolis cream, pure honey, or vitamin E. You can obtain vitamin E without the oil. Alternatively buy water-soluble vitamin E and prick the capsule to release the vitamin, then gently apply to the area.

Spots

For these, or any eruption of the skin, take zinc tablets and vitamin C, and cut out sugar and, especially, chocolate.

Thrush

Whether occurring in the mouth or the vagina, thrush can be alleviated or cured by taking Acidophilus and Pectin; also vitamin and mineral tablets and Amino Acid Complex.

Thyroid Gland

Whether the thyroid is over or under active, try the curative seaweed known as kelp. It contains iodine and many other minerals and is also a preventative.

Travel Sickness

Take ginger tablets from health stores or try Acidophilus.

Water Retention

Once more, try kelp. It is invaluable against this complaint.

Part Three

SURVIVING

Fifteen

DEATH – A NEW BEGINNING

I saw Eternity the other night
Like a great ring of pure and endless light,
All calm as it was bright;
And round beneath it, Time in hours,
days, years,
Driven by the spheres
Like a vast shadow moved; in which the world
And all her train were hurled.

Henry Vaughan (1622–95), 'The World'

SURVIVAL EVIDENCE

Here is a lovely story about my editor (who didn't really want the job in the first place, or so I tell him![1]). Often when we were working on this book he would come down to my house in Sussex and at lunchtime – which seemed to get earlier and earlier, for some reason! – we would adjourn for a drink and a bite at my local pub, a beautiful old hostelry, full of oak beams and not too crowded during the week.

One day something happened which my editor found quite extraordinary. We were sitting there

[1] I deny this! – Ed.

chatting and drinking our beer when I suddenly said: 'There's someone coming through. He says he wants to talk to you.'

EDITOR: Eh? You having me on?

BETTY: He's very insistent. He has a strong, rather rasping voice.

ED: How many beers have you had?

BETTY: Shut up and listen. Have you ever known a man called Eric?

ED: Well, I . . .

BETTY: He says he knew *you*. He's got a beaky nose . . . a rather strong, angular face . . . a—

ED: Good heavens, Eric. It's him to the life! Will he never stop interfering?

BETTY: He's very loquacious.

ED: Sounds just like you.

BETTY: I can't stop him talking.

ED: This is amazing. What's he saying?

BETTY: He's mentioning names. Len . . . Ralph . . .

ED: I knew a Len and a Ralph in journalism. Both great friends. What else?

BETTY: He's talking about this book. He says it's going to be a tremendous success.

ED: He always did have a sense of humour.

BETTY: He says you should be proud to be associated with it.

ED: What did I tell you?

BETTY: He says you had a pronounced musical gift but gave it up when you were young. Other things got in the way, apparently.

ED: Well, that's perfectly true. At least, I loved music,

270

especially the piano. But I gave up playing when I had to pass some exams for my next school. Typically spineless of me. Still, one of my sons is a professional pianist now, and that's a consolation. What else?

BETTY: He's mentioning more names. Kathy ... Blanche ...

That stopped the show for the moment. My editor wasn't sure what to think about Kathy — had he known a Kathy or not? But he was absolutely sure he'd never known a woman called Blanche.

Had I mistaken the name? A lot of the messages mediums receive get distorted by background noise, which makes it seem as though the message itself is not genuine, whereas what has occurred is a hearing error by the medium. But no. On this occasion I was certain I had heard right.

My editor was baffled. He was also quite startled. For this was his first experience of what is known as survival evidence — that is, of someone coming through to give messages after his or her death — and I believe that what the man who had spoken wanted, was to increase my editor's confidence in our enterprise by a personal demonstration of one of the things I would be talking about. What astonished my editor most of all was that this message should have come through, not in the quiet of my healing room but in the pub over a drink. But in fact this often happens. I have had some notable survival experiences in pubs and hotels; also, for some reason, at airports.

My editor was quite convinced that the man who

had come through was the man he had identified, and he told me that my description of his voice and appearance, as well as his remarks, tallied completely. I won't give the man's second name, at my editor's request. But he says that 'Eric', until his retirement and death a few years ago, was one of the great figures in the London book trade. He was tremendously influential. He liked his bottle of champagne in the journalists' wine bar, El Vino's in Fleet Street, and anyone in publishing over a certain age will know who I am talking about. I myself had never heard of the man, needless to say.

The only snags were 'Kathy' and 'Blanche', and it wasn't for another two weeks, when my editor was talking to a great friend of Eric's, who had looked after him when he was old and ill and pretty crotchety, that the mystery was solved. 'Kathy,' she said. 'Yes, he often called me that, just to tease me. It's a variant of my usual name. And Blanche – well, Blanche was the great love of his life!'

My editor rang me up straight away to tell me the news. 'Game, set and match to you, Betty,' he said.

Another remarkable man who decided to reappear was my own friend Ray Moore, the much-loved disc jockey whose dark-brown, velvet voice made thousands of weary souls feel that he was their closest friend. As all the world knows, Ray died of cancer of the mouth. He was one of those men who never think of themselves as brave, but I can tell you he was – extremely brave. He lived his life to the full and was loved by everyone who knew him, including myself.

I had actually never heard of Ray until I read an article in a Sunday newspaper which mentioned his cancer. I thought immediately: 'This man is going to telephone me' – and two hours later he did. What is even more extraordinary is that no sooner were we on the line than his late father came through, using me to communicate with him. This piece of survival evidence lasted about half an hour, with myself speaking the dead man's words into the mouthpiece. When our conversation ended the first thing Ray did, according to his wife Alma, was to pour himself a large glass of red wine! Typical Ray! On his first visit to my healing room he told me that everything his father had said to him had been correct in every detail.

At our first healing session Ray said he could feel about five pairs of hands all over him. For my part I could see the tumour being moved about and Ray could certainly feel it.

He said he experienced a feeling of total peace – although on his way home he felt as though a dozen knives were being used on him! Over the next six months he had many experiences that convinced him that there was life after the death of the physical body and that there were people in another dimension trying to help. Although he eventually died, the healing gave him much comfort and food for thought.

I taught Ray visualization techniques which enabled

him to raise his energy levels and partially leave his body. This eased the pain and the medical staff were amazed at how he managed for so much of the time to do without powerful drugs.

I first heard of his death on the television news. The next morning Alma telephoned to tell me the news herself and while we were talking Ray appeared by my side. I had never seen him without his beard, which he had grown to hide the growth. When I remarked on this to Alma she told me how much he had hated this beard.

Ray started to communicate with Alma through me during this telephone call and said: 'Please don't throw my cigarette case away.' Alma said, 'What on earth is he talking about a cigarette case for at a time like this?' Ray said that he had a special feeling for the case as it had been a presentation one, and that there was an inscription inside. Alma remembered, but thought it had been lost in one of their moves. We said goodbye.

About a month later I was asked to appear on a television programme to promote my book, *Mind to Mind*, and I asked Alma if she would take part in the programme. She agreed to do so, and when we met at the studio she produced the cigarette case. Inside was the badge of Ray's old station, ATV, which of course is now ITV. What Ray had been trying to say was that Alma was going to appear on ITV. It was his way of saying, 'Hey! There is no such thing as death.' As it happened, Pete Murray was on the same show, and Alma showed him the case and badge.

Two days before the memorial service being held for him, Ray appeared opposite to me, sitting in a chair, as I was having breakfast. He said: 'Betty, we've changed places. You're on the radio and I'm talking to the dead.' He was chuckling and smiling that wonderful smile of his. He asked me to relay some messages to Alma, which I did.

At his memorial service he was sitting cross-legged on the floor in front of the band! He hasn't appeared since. He probably thinks, 'If by this time I haven't convinced them that I've survived, I never will!' He is probably organizing things in another dimension.

I am telling Ray's story because so many thousands of people in Britain knew him and everything I have written about his appearance and character can be authenticated.

One last lovely story about him. He asked me to give Alma a single red rose when I met her for the memorial service. I ordered one but when it arrived it looked so pathetic that I bought her a bunch of red rosebuds at the station. I told Alma the story about the single red rose and apologized for not having carried out Ray's wishes. She said, 'Don't worry. He got through to someone else. I found a single red rose on my chair!'

This sort of evidence has been given through mediums for hundreds if not thousands of years. Why then do people still doubt? The knowledge that we survive the extinction of the physical body can release us all from the fear of death so that we can live our lives to the full. Make no mistake. Each of us is going to die. So why not learn and progress in this world so that we don't land up in the kindergarten department of the next?

Everything in the next dimension is constructed with the mind. That is why it is so important in this dimension to strengthen the mind with positive thought and imagination – then you will be up front when you die! You will not be lagging behind everyone else and take years to adapt. You will know exactly where you are going and what you want to achieve.

Death is birth. Both birth and death are traumatic. But as we survived the first, so surely shall we survive the second.

The mind is energy and when our physical body deteriorates and dies both its energy counterpart and its owner's mind energy leave and spin into another dimension. Although you are energy the dimension in which you will find yourself will be the same sort of energy so you will appear to be as solid as in this dimension. Everything is relative.

Michael Bentine's daughter, who was nicknamed Fusty, also died of cancer. She was a very beautiful girl. While Michael was having healing Fusty came through to give him a message about a house she had found for her parents. As they had been looking for years and still had not found one they liked, we were both rather surprised. She said her father wasn't to look for it – it would be given to him. And it would have an 'R' in the name.

Michael asked how he would recognize it. Fusty said he would know it as soon as he saw it.

We both thought this was all rather vague and I said: 'Come on Fusty, this sounds rather amateurish mediumship.' But she refused to say more.

A few weeks later Michael rang and said he had been offered a house and had fallen in love with it. There was no name. But he did look out of the top window and there, carved in the concrete, were the figures of the year in which the house had been built. It was the same year as Michael's birth! Michael hadn't relayed any of Fusty's messages to his wife Clementina but after they moved in she gave the house a name: Russell House!

Fusty appeared once more to me. It was my birthday, but for all that I was feeling very tired and down. She said: 'Come on Betty, enjoy yourself. It's your birthday.' When I told Michael, he said that was typical. She always insisted that people should enjoy their birthdays.

You see, people do not change. What you are at death you continue to be. You do not become a different being. You continue to be yourself. Whether you like it or not.

If you are still not sure whether to believe or not, try turning the whole situation the other way around. Imagine you are on the other side and somebody tells you: 'When you are born you will go down this dark tunnel (the birth canal) into bright lights where there will be people waiting for you. They will guide you and protect you until such a time as you are able to look after yourself. There will be schools and universities but you will only go to the latter if you have acquired enough knowledge.' This would sound very way out, but, as you know, it is true. What is the difficulty, then, in believing in other worlds while you are here?

Knowledge is the only way to progress, in whatever dimension. Seeking it strengthens the mind and enables you to achieve. The mind is everlasting. The body is merely a tube which we inhabit in this dimension and which will later be dispensed with. It plays a very small part really when you compare the time we live in it with the everlasting quality of the mind and the different dimensions and universes we could find ourselves in! I think death is extremely exciting and, when it is near, what a fantastic journey we have to look forward to!

Those of you who will never believe are living your lives in a sea of negativity. If we are not going anywhere, then everything we have learned will be wasted. In that case, there would be no purpose in the universe at all. Nothing in it would make sense. We play such a small part in the theatre of the universe and even that minor part would be a waste of time if we didn't survive. Think about it! None of it would make any sense at all!

Do you really think that the architect of planets and universes would be so stupid as to create minds that would only survive for a fraction of time? What an idiotic waste that would be!

I once taught a boy of thirteen, who was dying of cancer, how to leave his body and ease the pain. It was the balloon exercise described at the beginning

278

of this book. When he actually died he told a friend he was going to jump into Betty's balloon. He died very peacefully. He had also received many messages from his grandmother who was dead and he knew that he was going somewhere else to start a new life. The fact that he himself had received this survival evidence enabled him to come back and give some in return, only a few months after his death. A few weeks before Christmas he appeared in my lounge and asked if I would telephone his mother and tell her to wear the necklace he had bought for her the previous Christmas. I passed on the message and his mother confirmed that he had, indeed, bought her a pendant necklace that Christmas. How could I know this? His parents had been with him every time he came to see me and we never discussed small items of this kind. How can people not believe when this sort of evidence crops up every day through the work of many mediums?

At the time of this boy's death another of my patients, a young man of nineteen, died of a brain tumour. He appeared to me before his funeral and asked me to telephone his mother, which I did. Communicating through me he described his home at Christmas, a red rose that was still in a little vase, the copper vase full of chrysanthemums. He reproached his mother with no longer cooking properly, as she used to. After all, he said, there was the rest of the family to think of. He was also cross with her for letting her hair go and for not buying a new raincoat. She told me he was always like this. She laughed and added (it was the day before his funeral): 'Well, I beat him to that. I bought a new mac this morning!'

Needless to say this telephone call brought great joy. What other proofs of the mind's survival do we need?

I had talked to both these boys about mind energy: how to expand it and link it up with other energies and so to rejuvenate themselves. They asked me questions all the time about dying and I explained that when the body was beyond healing the mind released itself and spun into an energy dimension. They were always fascinated and our conversations were happy and totally positive. There was also quite a lot of leg pulling on both sides.

I was sad at losing them. I loved them both. But to have them reappear and prove not only to their families but also to me that what I am teaching is the truth is a bonus and I thank them for it.

I have thought about the messages I have received over the years and they have always been positive. My clients, however, are sometimes far from positive and there are days when my own positivity is at a low ebb. Yet still I receive tremendously powerful positive information and help. This help has to come from someone with a personality quite distinct from and outside my own and that of my clients. Its style is too independent.

The incredible detail of these messages is also astonishing. Again, the personality has to be distinct, because the information I receive is full of detail that neither I nor my clients had known before. They had to go away and find out from family or friends (as my editor did) whether the information was correct. It is *always* correct!

Besides proof of mind survival there is also evidence that the mind leaves the body during sleep. Children who have been to see me, and many who have not, have described me to their parents. The children who had visited me have merely said: 'It was that lady I saw the other day.' Those who had not visited me but whom I had been asked to help were able to describe my physical appearance – features and so on – in detail. But all of them said that I was either wearing a long white dress or a blue one. I obviously have another wardrobe somewhere that isn't costing me a penny!

Certainly we should listen to children more often than we do. Many of them have psychic experiences before the age of seven and sometimes later. Up to that age they have time for day-dreaming, which, far from being the time-wasting activity that many people think, is actually what releases the mind energy and enables the child to contact the next dimension. Once school work starts there is obviously less time for this – more's the pity.

We should all day-dream more than we do. It releases the mind energy and allows us to absorb information and healing from another source. It takes the pressure off the brain and body and enables the body to breathe, the blood to circulate and major organs to vibrate instead of being clamped into a dense mass of negative energy.

But if you cannot day-dream you can at least allow yourself moments of dawdling when you appear to be doing nothing. Do not reproach yourself with this. Any escape is better than none, if it helps to release the mind energy.

Another experience I have had when I am healing children is telepathy. Children pick up my mind energy while at home – which can sometimes be hundreds of miles away – and they will tell me when they next visit me what I have been doing and what I have been eating and will draw for me pictures of all sorts of things that have nothing to do with their lives but a lot to do with mine. Obviously these impressions are picked up while I am giving them absent healing and they remember them. So here is yet another example of how the mind energy can travel and link up with other minds.

Which reminds me of an incident that occurred three years ago. I was giving healing to a man, a stranger to me at that time, and I had to interrupt the healing because a little girl (a spirit girl, that is) appeared at my side and asked if I would give a message to her father. I asked the man if he knew anyone who had lost a little girl and he said no. I then asked if it was his little girl but he said he had no children and never had had any. The little girl continued talking to me and told me that her daddy was very unhappy because she had died and she wanted to tell him that she wasn't dead and that she was with her grandmother. She mentioned a motor bike in connection with her grandmother but it didn't make sense.

The little girl continued talking and I remembered everything she said and also the dress she appeared to be wearing. When the healing session had finished I said to my client: 'This little girl has appeared because you know her father.' This he denied, but after he had gone I telephoned a mutual friend – I was determined to get to the bottom of the mystery – and the friend told me that there was a man in the same street who had lost a little girl and was distraught about it. So I described the little girl and my description exactly fitted.

Now at last I was getting somewhere! Later I discovered that the man who was having healing from me had indeed visited the little girl's house and had met her father, but only once, and had evidently forgotten the occasion – at least, at the time of the healing he failed to make the link. It also appeared that the little girl's grandmother had been killed by a motor cycle. The child knew this, and referred to it at the healing, but her father had told nobody else.

This story is remarkable because it shows to what lengths dead people will go to ease the pain of those who loved them by proving that they still exist. At the time this child came through neither my client nor myself had any idea who she was, so there was certainly no question of telepathic communication.

There is so much evidence and yet sceptics will go to great lengths to deny it. Why? Surely such an attitude is totally negative and also quite pointless.

Many of my readers have heard me on Pete Murray's talk-back show on LBC. Many of the people who phone in to this programme tell of their own experiences of actually seeing 'dead' relatives. One lady woke up to find her husband in bed with her – and looking very much alive! For a few minutes she actually forgot that he had died. Another listener told of things moving about in her house since a son had died. This is one of the ways the dead have of bringing to our attention the fact that they are still around. What they would like to say is: 'Hey! I'm still around, even if you can't see me.' There are so many different stories but the message is always the same: 'I'm still living!'

How many more stories and how many more years will it take to convince people that we really do still live on?

Another thing that has appalled me since my first book *Mind to Mind* was published is how some journalists (a small minority, happily) continually get their facts wrong as well as inventing a lot of rubbish – remarks that I am supposed to have made but never did!

However clearly and concisely I try to describe my work I still have reporters saying, 'Has he shaved his beard off since he died?' or 'Why did she appear in that dress?' or – another classic – 'Surely they don't have steak and kidney pies over there?' It seems that after hearing how people who have died project an image of themselves, and how they remember themselves with their likes and dislikes (though this, remember, is still only a projected image, not the full reality of those people as they were) some journalists still want to make it all sound ridiculous. Well, that is their privilege, but they will have to deal with the consequences – and those consequences may surprise them! Intelligent people understand totally. Indeed they may well have had comparable experiences of their own.

When a group of people get together and the subject of life after death arises it is amazing how many stories are told once someone has broken the ice. It seems that people are so afraid of being laughed at that they keep their experiences to themselves. Being psychic is normal. It is those who aren't psychic who are abnormal, because they have lost what should be a very normal gift. Animals in the wild are psychic. It is only domesticated animals who have lost the gift. Except, of course, cats, who live on their wits and are so independent that their psychic abilities are still intact. Cats are able to find their way back to their old house when they have been moved to a new one hundreds of miles away. A dog, too, still has the ability to see spirits. Whenever spirit people are around you will see a dog staring at them until they disappear. I have seen not only my dogs doing this but those of my friends too.

Please do not go through life believing that when you die everything ends. This destroys the pleasure you should have in your present existence; it also discourages you from seeking knowledge and strengthening your mind energy. Death is a new beginning and something to look forward to when this life ends. In the meantime, make sure you live this one to the full and do not allow fear of death or anything else to spoil it. Life is for living, whatever dimension you may find yourself in.

Perhaps you would like to contact someone you have lost. It is quite easy. Simply sit down and close your eyes or, if you prefer, wait until you go to bed so that you are really comfortable and relaxed. Then simply think of the person you would like to speak to. Make sure you have a clear picture or at least that you are feeling completely convinced that the person is there.

Now pass on your thoughts to that person telepathically. In all cases speak to the people with whom you wish to communicate as though they were in the room with you and as though you were speaking verbally and out loud. When you have finished communicating, sit or lie quietly and listen. You will hear an audible silence but within that silence there will be a message. At first you will not know what the message is, but the next day you will find yourself inspired in one way or another or will simply discover that the answers to your problems have been given to you. Practice makes perfect and after several communications things will begin to get easier. But be assured from the start that you will know, without the shadow of a doubt, that this is so.

I, as a medium, can already receive messages. By being positive all your life and expanding your mind energy you will find that you also are becoming more intuitive, if not mediumistic. One word of warning, though. Do not become obsessed with the desire to communicate; that would only be negative. Seek to obtain survival evidence, or other similar experiences, only when you really need to.

Recently one of my clients brought a friend of his along with him. This friend was a sceptic. But when, during the healing, his father came through and started to give him survival evidence, he was dumbstruck, because the detail contained in the evidence was so convincing. Then his father asked him if he remembered their neighbour, a lady called Alice. He didn't remember her. The healing session ended and both the men left.

When my client next came for his healing he told me the sequel. It seems that as they drove home his friend got on his car telephone and rang up his mother, who lived in Birmingham. He asked her some details about his own early life and it appeared that everything his father had said was accurate. Then he asked: 'Do you remember the name of our neighbour when I was a youngster?' His mother said she couldn't and he felt very frustrated. But when he reached home his mother phoned him back. She said: 'I remember her now. Her name was Alice!'

It is interesting when clients arrive for their appointment and upon opening the door I see a 'spirit' walk in with them. It is as though they have been escorted to their destination. At once the 'spirit' begins to communicate, usually confirming that it has brought about the meeting so that important information can be passed on.

It is remarkable how this is done. The mind of the deceased person connects up with the minds of people who are in contact with the person with whom it wishes to communicate; alternatively, it may go straight to the person and urge him or her to seek out a medium.

I have listened to so many incredible stories. One day a lady arrived on my doorstep and said, 'I don't even know why I'm here, I was speaking to a woman in America about ordinary, everyday things and she suddenly dived into her handbag, produced a pen and wrote down your address, saying, "If you are ever in England do go and see this lady." When I asked her why, she said, "You will know when you get there," and that was that. I don't even know who you are!'

I laughed and explained that I was a medium and healer. I said, 'I don't think you need healing but please come in.' Fortunately on that day I had some free time, which was unusual!

We sat down and immediately a young man started to communicate. It was her son, who had died in a car accident. The evidence was quite extraordinary. Afterwards my visitor said, 'I wasn't meant to know what you did because my son knew I would never have visited you. I have been against this sort of thing all my life.'

I asked her how she could be against something she knew nothing about. It's rather like finding someone guilty of a crime before you have investigated the evidence. She smiled, 'Yes, it's stupid isn't it!' When she left she told me the meeting had changed her life, that now she could continue with her own life and let go of the grief. 'There is no way that it couldn't have been my son. You even had his mannerisms.' We said our goodbyes. There is no doubt that there is far more going on behind the scenes than we ever dream of.

So many people cannot bear to think of their friends and family being buried underground or being cremated. There is no need for these upsetting emotions. When the body ceases to function the mind leaves – indeed, it has practically left weeks before the death. Ever vibrant, it still lives on, albeit in another dimension. To remember this also makes living a whole lot easier.

I could write a whole book about survival evidence, most of it quite extraordinary in the exactness of its detail. But if what you have read so far has failed to convince you, then perhaps you will never believe. In that case, so be it. But please do not block other people's positivity by insisting that you are right. You never know, you could be wrong!

OUT OF BODY EXPERIENCES

So much has been written about Out of Body Experiences – which from now on I shall just call OOBE – and yet many people are still unsure what to make of the subject. So I hope the following accounts of cases, all taken from within my own personal range of knowledge, will give you a clearer idea of what occurs and what it all means.

First of all, let me tell you about a builder who came to me for healing. He had suffered two heart attacks and he came to me for two reasons. First, he thought I could give him peace of mind, if not a cure. Secondly, he hoped I could give him the sort of ease that would enable him to leave his body quickly when the time came for him to go. What he told me when he first came to me was of great interest.

He said that when he had had his first attack he found himself looking down at his physical body on the bed. He found that he could look down at his body from all angles but he also felt rather dreamy, as though he had been tranquillized. The whole experience was uncannily enjoyable, with a feeling of complete calm and peace. Then suddenly he felt himself being drawn back into his own body and the awful heart pain began once more.

When he had his second attack he found himself once again detached from his physical body, but this time travelling at great speed down a tunnel at the end of which he saw his dead father. His father greeted him and said: 'It isn't time yet. You must go back.' Whereupon he found himself looking down at his body from ceiling height and saw the medical team giving it electric shocks. He saw his body jumping around but didn't feel a thing. He said he wanted to tell the doctors not to bother as he was happy as he was. Then suddenly, again, he found himself back in his body and was so furious he swore at the doctors, asking what they thought they were doing and why he couldn't be left in peace. This patient lived another two years, then suffered a third and massive heart attack which proved fatal.

Every time this builder visited me I was impressed by the fact that he had lost all fear of dying. His actual words were: 'How can I be afraid of death when I actually saw my father and he spoke to me? There was no way my father was dead. He was very much alive.'

When I told him about my studies of mind energy, how by thought it can be projected anywhere in the world, and how at death it leaves the body and goes into another dimension, he replied: 'You are absolutely right. I have experienced what you say.' He also told me he had found a way of relieving pain by thinking about the sensations he had had while floating around the ceiling, spinning through the tunnel, and meeting his father. He said: 'It seemed as though I could project myself halfway into a sort of dream world where there was no pain.' What he was really doing, of course, was expanding his mind energy so that it was halfway out of his body, relieving the pressure of negative energies and also repositioning his energy counterpart so that it had no feeling.

I also have had this sort of experience many times, especially when I first wake up. Although on these occasions my eyes are open I cannot move a single muscle and I feel no bodily sensations at all. The first time this happened I thought I was paralysed and the fear quickly brought my mind energy and energy counterpart back into alignment.

In fact, I have since found that this is quite a common occurrence. At any rate, a surprising number of people I have talked to about it seem to have experienced something similar, and since my first book was published a lot of the letters I have received have been from readers telling me about their own OOBE. No wonder the information in that book made sense to them – and in this one too, I hope! But there are also some people who persist, for whatever reason, in pretending to find the whole thing completely incredible.

Incidentally, you should also remember that when patients are in a coma they can still be aware of everything that is going on around them. Many people have talked about their experiences while in this state, how they have seen family around them and have heard snatches of conversation. Some have heard nurses say: 'There's no hope', and they have wanted to shout: 'Hey! I'm still here!' The reason for this is that the mind, having been shocked almost completely out of the body, is still slightly attached and aware of its physical surroundings.

It is therefore very important, when dealing with comatose patients, to be positive, happy and optimistic. This mood will be absorbed by them and help them to recover.

I had another thirteen-year-old patient whom I also taught to go out into the universe in his air balloon when he was in pain. He was dying of bone cancer among other things. This is what he told me:

'When I was going out into space I couldn't feel any more pain and I could see other people passing by but they weren't in air balloons or anything and they didn't seem to know I was there because they were looking straight ahead. Then I was floating around the ceiling and looking down on my body and I saw a nurse come in and look at me and take my pulse. She rushed out of the room and another nurse came and took my pulse and then I was back in my body but no-one was in the room and then they rushed back in and said: "You gave us a fright. Where have you been?" They then sat me up and gave me a sip of water but I was feeling fine.'

I have heard the same story, in different forms, again and again. Doctors and scientists all over the world have been studying this phenomenon and some have admitted that there do seem to be people who can leave their bodies at will and return at will. But it takes courage for a member of the medical establishment to admit this – and even more to agree that perhaps we do indeed survive death. But I know this happens because I have been leaving my body since I was two years old. Because I have what is called a loose astral body (that is, my energy counterpart and mind energy are able to leave my body very easily), this body would formerly leave my physical body at whim, so to speak, but now I can control it. I still have very spiritual experiences when I leave my body but mostly I use this gift for very sick patients who may be on the other side of the world or who I think may benefit from my actual spirit presence. Many people have seen me by their bedside, as I have mentioned before in this book, but I am unaware of this myself when it occurs while I am sleeping.

If you find OOBE occurring without undue effort on your part, then you have no need to worry about the consequences. If, however, you are forcing yourself to achieve these experiences, then I believe you are taking big risks. An OOBE should be a natural happening after you have trained your mind to leave and return to your body in response to a single, swift thought. In fact, when you have learned to do this in an effortless way you will find the experience so wonderful that you will certainly want to try out variations. Imagination is the key to the universe. It is easy and safe to take partial leave of your body and when you wish it you simply think yourself back. I repeat, however: don't force it. Just so long as it happens naturally it is all quite safe, and extremely spiritual.

REINCARNATION

All the evidence I have makes me believe without a doubt that we return after death to inhabit another physical body. It may be several years later. It may be only one year! But so many people are still so sceptical about this belief that I wonder what they are frightened of. Are they afraid to come back to a planet that we have so horribly polluted? I shouldn't be surprised. I'm not particularly thrilled myself at the idea that I may be obliged to come back and help to clean up the mess! At all events, many people – a majority, in all likelihood – refuse to believe that we return, and some get quite hot under the collar when their view is contradicted.

One man wrote to me after hearing me on Pete Murray's talkback programme, on which I am privileged to respond to many people's problems and fears: 'I love your programme, but when you started talking about reincarnation I became angry. I thought you had more sense.' What will he have thought if he watched, as I hope he did, an edition soon afterwards of the programme *40 Minutes* that was entirely devoted to the subject?

In this remarkable programme a little girl testified about her former life, which she recalled in great detail from a very early age. Another extraordinary witness, a six-year-old Indian boy called Titu, talked about the radio shop he had owned in the town of Agra, in his previous incarnation, only a few years before. Then he had been a young man called Suresh Verma. Now, with his new parents, he was living about twelve miles away, in a small village. The boy described his death in that previous incarnation – how he had been shot in the temple by another young man as he was driving home in his car. Sure enough the local records, which the *40 Minutes* team looked up, contained Suresh's death certificate authenticating the fatal wound. Titu, the programme established, has what looks like a birthmark in exactly the same place.

Titu described his shop, his then wife, Uma, and his two children. In fact there was very little about his former life that he did not remember in detail. The *40 Minutes* team took their cameras along to film him in the radio shop. 'You have changed things around,' he told Suresh's widow. 'One side is different from before. Those units have also been added.' Uma said all this was correct. Titu was also asked to point out Suresh's children, who were playing with some friends outside. This he not only did but he also knew their names.

Remember, this little boy Titu was only six years old and his children from his former existence were not much older, so there could only have been an interval of a few years at most between his death and his reincarnation. Whatever questions were put to him he answered correctly and the evidence for reincarnation produced by this interview was surely overwhelming. Uma believes. Suresh's father believes. The situation, in fact, is only sad for Titu's parents, because they feel that his old life attracts him so much that as he gets older he will try to go back to it. A swami has explained to them: 'It depends on how much love and affection you are able to give him. That will influence him most.'[1]

Some time ago I read about a little girl who had been murdered (her throat had been cut) as a baby in her former existence and who still bears the scars in this one. Though now an American she remembers that she had lived in India and told her mother about the house she used to live in and the colour it was painted.

All these children remember their past lives very vividly and begin to talk about them as soon as they can speak. A scientist who was very interested in reincarnation asked the mother's permission to take this last child back to the village in India that she so constantly spoke about and when they arrived the child pointed out the house she used to live in and said they had changed the colour of it outside. They knocked at the door, which was opened by a lady who the little girl said was her mother and who agreed that the colour of the outside of the house had indeed been changed – and from the colour the child had mentioned. The scientist then took the little girl into the village where she pointed to an old man. 'It was he who murdered me,' she said.

So many stories point to the fact of reincarnation – those I have quoted are a mere handful. They incidentally prove my point that the survival evidence given by mediums is genuine and not a variety

[1]*Psychic News* carried a detailed report of this memorable programme.

of thought transference, as many would have us believe. I myself have received many messages that prove, without a shadow of doubt, that the mind survives.

Many people, having sought out a medium for the specific purpose of communicating with a relative or friend, feel bitterly let down when that person does not come through. What they fail to realize is that the person they hoped to hear from may already be inhabiting another body. This could be the body of their nephew or niece; their mother could be their own daughter; their uncle could be their son. For the evidence shows that, strange though it may seem, we do tend, apparently, to reincarnate in groups. Even if the person is no longer of your own family, he or she may not be far away, as in the case of the Indian boy.

If there were no such thing as the survival of the mind, how can I see spirits and have the power to describe them? I have no idea what somebody's grandmother looked like, and yet I can describe people in detail – colour of hair and eyes, shape of nose, and whether they were short or tall, fat or thin. How could I do this if I was not seeing that person? But the mind does survive and the people I describe are projecting a mirror image of themselves as they now remember themselves when they were in this dimension.

Some people don't want to survive because of the awful life they have had this time round. Who can blame them? But the next dimension is very different to this one. Your mind is the same, but the place where you will find yourself will be far more caring, the colours will be more vivid, and you yourself will have the change of living and improving your mind in an unpolluted environment. I have always felt that this planet must be on one of the lowest planes of life. Yet we are obviously here for a purpose and there is no opting out until it is time for us to go on.

What has struck me most in all the years that I have been passing on evidence of survival is that no one has ever expressed a wish to return to this earth. All say they would *never* return, given the choice. If that is the case, then the next dimension should hold no fears.

For this reason also I think it is sad that the media so often seem to sensationalize mediumship, clairvoyance and healing. All these are perfectly natural gifts and good mediums do not go about with beads around their heads and wearing flowing gowns. Most of them are busy as well as very positive people whose role as they see it is to bring consolation to those who have lost family and friends and whose religion they feel, for whatever reason, has let them down.

But don't take my word for it. Investigate the subject for yourself. There is no shortage of material. Just do not dismiss what I have written out of hand. Who knows – one day you may find out that I was right!

All these stories may appear very strange and perhaps you are wondering, why is she telling them to us? It is because, as I have already said and emphasized several times, this book has been written to help you along your own path. You yourself may have such experiences in the future, or even stranger ones, entirely personal to yourself. How can you tell what experiences you could have unless you expand your mind energy and give them the chance to materialize?

MEDIUMS

As a conclusion to this chapter I would like to write something about mediums, since so many people have so many misconceptions about them. Not all of us, contrary to popular belief, are old women sitting in darkened rooms, wearing voluminous robes and thinking up tricks to play on the unsuspecting public!

I myself have moved on from giving sittings. Having discovered mind energy I now feel it important to concentrate on this because I could see that, by teaching control of this energy, I can bring others total independence. Nowadays I also shy away from clairvoyance as far as I can. I find that when you tell people what is likely to occur they are inclined to sit back and stop doing things for themselves. Since one of the leading principles of my life – and of this book – is that all of us can and should be self-reliant, such a passive frame of mind is the last thing I want to encourage! At any rate, in all cases I speak from a position of knowledge, as the discovery and study of mind energy are entirely unique to myself.

Mediums work in a number of different ways, according to their different gifts. One of the most remarkable I have known is Leslie Flint, the voice medium. His helpers construct a voice box from ectoplasm (life force) through which the dead can communicate by means of their earthly voice. What happens is that their mind projects a memory of what their earthly voice sounded like, which produces the sound itself, for sound is vibration and the mind, being of a vibrational nature, can mimic any sound it likes. Tapes have been made of Leslie Flint's sessions over forty years and the friends and families of countless of those who have spoken through him have recognized the voices and testified that they are genuine. Alas, there are no young voice mediums to take Leslie's place and this, to him, is a great sadness.

The late Helen Duncan was a physical, or materialization, medium, probably one of the most extraordinary who ever lived. She used to sit in a small cubicle and go into a trance and the spirits who appeared clothed themselves in ectoplasm which emanated from her, with the result that all those present could recognize their friends or relatives, shake their hands and hug them. Ectoplasm is the medium's energy or life force and can be seen under an infra-red glow. It is like grey muslin, and creeps along the ground to be absorbed by the spirits standing there, which then gradually become solid. When it begins to return to the medium the spirits dematerialize, usually from the legs up. But, of course, they are still there.

Charles Horrey, the man who told me I was going to be a medium, sat with Helen Duncan many times. On one occasion a dead friend of his appeared. He said, 'Hello, Charles, lovely to see you again,' and gave him a hug and a kiss. He felt solid but just a little bit cold, Horrey told me. Then he said: 'Got to go now, but you can see there's no such thing as death.'

A medium like myself can see these entities without their being absorbed into the ectoplasm and materializing. But to me the greatest sadness is that the whole world cannot see them because if they did they would know that our minds survive.

The point to remember is that when people move into the next dimension they feel as solid as they did in this and are as easily seen, because their energies match it on the vibrational level. (Incidentally, I think it is also worth making the point that mediums do not operate on the level of 'ordinary' sensitivity, but of 'vibrational' sensitivity.)

When I think of such things, and of the freedom that comes after death, I realize that one of the most frustrating things about this physical body of ours is that we've only got two little portholes to look through – our eyes. That is why it is so important to expand our mind energy as far as we possibly can. Then we literally 'see' with our minds. When I am giving survival evidence the dead are attaching their minds to mine. That enables them to imprint pictures on my own mind so that I can describe them. For instance, one spirit visitor gave me a description of the house she lived in, probably back in the 1930s. It was a little terraced house with a little back yard, old-fashioned grate with a fender round it on which socks were drying. Her granddaughter told me that this was certainly her house, and that that was exactly the style she lived in.

Helen Duncan had an eventful and tragic life. In 1933 she was charged with fraud and in 1944, towards the end of the Second World War, was sentenced under the Witchcraft Act of 1735. Finally she died of shock after police burst into a house in Nottingham where she was conducting a seance, interrupted the proceedings, and grabbed hold of her. Interrupting any seance carries grave danger to the medium, in this case fatal danger. This is because the life force has gone out temporarily from the medium's body and when it comes rushing back, the suddenness with which it does so can cause injury or even death. Hence the need to have people guarding the doors, and taking every other precaution.

Then there are trance mediums. These just sit quietly with their eyes closed and allow somebody else's mind to come in and take the place of their own energy and thus take them over. At that point the medium will physically assume the visitor's appearance.

George Chapman is entranced by a deceased surgeon called William Lang, who once worked at

London's Middlesex Hospital. That is, the medium while he is working, is taken over by this spirit doctor. Although George Chapman gives healing for every type of sickness, he is famous for his astonishing cures for eye ailments.

I took a friend of mine to see him before I became a healer myself. Because my friend was nervous I was allowed to go into the surgery with him. As Doctor Lang started to work, he looked at my friend and said: 'I don't know why you have come to me. You have brought a healer with you.'

It was a memorable moment for me.

There are several other kinds of mediums, and several other kinds of manifestations. Rosemary Brown, through whom famous composers work, was chosen because she is not a musical academic, so that the composers can come through with their own personalities while she writes down the notes. Other automatic writing occurs in the same way: a personality, known or unknown, 'dictates'. The medium just writes the words down.

I myself am a mind medium. I receive messages and pass them on by word of mouth. I hear the voice of the person speaking – the exact voice, with its accent, pitch and intonation all absolutely correct and clear. Sometimes the person positively yells at me. The other day, for instance, I was with a patient and as I came through the door to give her a cup of tea I heard a woman's voice shouting: 'Tell her it's Marjorie!' She shouted it three times and I thought, well, I can't ignore her. So I passed on the message.

After that, the woman went on speaking for about an hour. It was absolutely astonishing the amount of information she gave my patient about her family – and all of it accurate. In fact, she was my patient's mother-in-law, and her words came out so fast that in order to capture them, my patient had to take them down in shorthand. She said to me afterwards: 'Betty, you are obviously right about these voices. I know all the people she was talking about and what she said was completely correct.'

I mentioned earlier the strange-seeming fact that a lot of survival evidence has come through to me in pubs, especially old pubs, possibly because so many powerful energies have been left behind in the fabric of such places. Being clairvoyant, I only have to touch the brickwork and I begin to form a picture of the inn as it once was.

As this has been rather a serious chapter, here is a lighthearted story about one of these hostelries, where I used to 'see' clairvoyantly a large man, with a watch chain across his front, leaning against the bar. 'That was my father,' the proprietress told me. 'Do you ever see him when you come in in the evening?' 'No,' I replied. 'That's right,' she replied. 'He never sat here in the evenings.' There was also one very old inn near my home where, every time I took people there, survival evidence of one kind or another seemed to take place.

I tell these stories, first and foremost, to comfort and reassure the many people who are frightened of death. This is a tragic situation. Many people are so worried about what will happen when they die, and about when they are going to die, that they give themselves no chance to enjoy this present dimension, this life as we have it now. In short, people are so frightened of death that they are afraid to live. It is tragic too when a person with a terminal illness says: 'I am going to die. There is nothing afterwards. What have I done with my life?' My intention in this book has been to show you that the mind survives, and to help you to strengthen your mind in this dimension to such an extent that you will achieve great things in the next. Yet again, mind energy is the key.

All mediums must have expansive mind energies, and be positive when they are at work. Otherwise they would not be able to link up with the energy dimension. And it is a mind energy we should all share. Most people are so inhibited that they live in mental prisons. They refuse to allow their minds to expand for fear of being thought peculiar, or even mental, by so-called normal people. In fact of course, it's the 'normal' people who are abnormal, having submerged so much of the potential we all possess, and the 'peculiar' ones who are normal. The 'normal' people shouldn't be listened to anyway, if all they can do is to be dismissive and derisive. They have too much negativity.

My proofs are positive and they leave me with two aims: to help to rid people of the fear of dying and to comfort the grieving families and friends of the deceased or the terminally ill. Dying is often a painful process but if, at the end, there is another beginning, where our mind is free and the crippled or disease-ridden body is no longer necessary, then it can also be a joy.

Finally, the medium must take a firm line about the messages that come through. When I first started practising I got some weird ones. I finally said: 'Look, if you can't talk sense, don't bother to come through at all!'

I received no further messages for about six months, then they began again, and from then on they were intelligent. They were meaningful and comforting to those for whom they were intended. That is how mediums should develop their mediumship, but too few of them seem to have the courage to do so today – perhaps that was always the case. You have to take the risk that you will receive nothing more.

With the help of this book I know your courage will never fail you again and you will go forward with greater positivity and a feeling of well-being that you will want to keep for ever.

LAST WORD

In the past twenty years I have covered a lot of unknown territory. My courage, spirituality and positivity have been examined under a microscope by my many unseen friends in other dimensions. I seem to have passed their test – at least, they are still endowing me with spiritual gifts so that I can, as a teacher, pass them on to others.

Knowledge, especially spiritual knowledge, is not for a chosen few. It is for everyone. And in this book I have tried to pave the way for you, making the path easier and yet not too easy, for there is no way you can progress without putting in a lot of effort. Having made that effort, however, you will be ready to move up – to higher things and higher levels. I am not saying that when we reach these levels we shall become what is commonly thought of as 'saints'. That would be difficult in this dimension, where at all times our feet must be kept firmly on the ground. But the benefits to be gained from the methods I have described are in all ways immense. We become, in the first place, healthier – one of the greatest boons of all. We become more loving and understanding, because of our growth in sensitivity.

We become more successful, more independent, and, above all, more courageous.

Never again, from this stage onwards, will you allow people to dominate your life, to humiliate you, to ill-treat you, or to break your heart. Henceforth they will enter your life on equal terms, because you will insist that they respect you for what you are, and most of all for your mind, which it must be your life's work, in all humility, to enlarge.

If you have followed all the exercises and advice in this book you don't need me to tell you this. If you haven't reached the stage I am talking about, then go back and read the book again and again until you do. The feeling of permanent freedom is worth all the effort.

I am still reaping the spiritual rewards for the effort I have put into my life. It has been extremely difficult most of the time – but then, fortunately, nobody told me that it would be easy, not even my mother! I no longer expect to receive happiness without pain, to be loved without loving, to succeed without hard work.

Becoming an explorer of other dimensions is sometimes fraught but always exciting. I know that, hidden in the folds of the Tapestry of the Universe, there are millions of secrets. Maybe I will only find a few, and that with great effort, by continuing to unravel that tapestry thread by thread.

I also know that I will never give up – in other words, I'm hooked. I shall go on until it's time for me to leave this dimension and join another. What a journey that will be. But while I am here I will never be bored. That would be a living death!

Doris Collins, that great medium and healer, told me many years ago that I would heal through the written word. At the time I was working as a medium and healer seventy-eight hours a week, and had been doing so for ten years. My dearest wish had always been to write a book about my experiences but I could not believe, at that time, there was any way that this could happen. She also said that my name would be known all over the world and that my books would be a success. This promise kept me going when I wanted to give up out of sheer frustration and exhaustion. I'm glad I didn't and I would like to thank her for the time she gave me, for her wonderful mediumship, and for her understanding when I needed it most.

I have now become dedicated to healing through the written word, and although I can no longer give private consultations, you, the reader, will have all the help you need in the privacy of your own home when you read this book and when you link up with me by thought. That is what 'Mind Magic' means.

Many years ago I came across a poem by an anonymous Maori warrior which I have loved ever since. It sums up all I believe and I hope you find it as beautiful as I do. It is my parting present to you, my reader. Here it is.

MY LAW – TIEME RANAPIRI

The sun may be clouded, yet ever the sun
Will sweep on its course till the Cycle is run.
And when into chaos the system is hurled
Again shall the Builder reshape a new world.

Your path may be clouded, uncertain your goal:
Move on – for your orbit is fixed to your soul.
And though it may lead into darkness of night
The torch of the Builder shall give it new light.

You were. You will be! Know this while you are:
Your spirit has travelled both long and afar.
It came from the Source, to the Source it returns –
The Spark which was lighted eternally burns.

It slept in a jewel. It leapt in a wave.
It roamed in the forest. It rose from the grave.
It took on strange garbs for long aeons of years
And now in the soul of yourself It appears.

From body to body your spirit speeds on
It seeks a new form when the old one has gone
And the form that it finds is the fabric you wrought
On the loom of the Mind from the fibre of Thought.
As dew is drawn upwards, in rain to descend
Your thoughts drift away and in Destiny blend.
You cannot escape them, for petty or great,
Or evil or noble, they fashion your Fate.

Somewhere on some planet, sometime and
  somehow
Your life will reflect your thoughts of your Now.
My Law is unerring, no blood can atone –
The structure you built you will live in – alone.
From cycle to cycle, through time and through
  space
Your lives with your longings will ever keep pace
And all that you ask for, and all you desire
Must come at your bidding, as flame out of fire.

Once list' to that Voice and all tumult is done –
Your life is the Life of the Infinite One.
In the hurrying race you are conscious of pause
With love for the purpose, and love for the Cause.

You are your own Devil, you are your own God
You fashioned the paths your footsteps have trod.
And no-one can save you from Error or Sin
Until you have hark'd to the Spirit within.

Attributed to a Maori

Bibliography

Benham, William G., *Laws of Scientific Hand Reading*, Tarporevala, Bombay, 1975

Bhaktivendanta, Swami Prabhupada, *Bhagavad Gita*, Bhaktivendanta Book Trust, London and Sydney, 1968

Davies, Dr Stephen and Stewart, Dr Alan, *Nutritional Medicine*, Pan Books. London and Sydney, 1987

Deshpande, P. Y., *The Authentic Yoga*, Rider & Company, London, 1982

Erdmann, Dr Robert and Jones, Meiron, *The Amino Revolution*, Century Publishing Company, London, 1987

Garde, Dr R. K. *Yoga Therapy*, Wolfe, New Delhi, 1973

Harris, Bertha, *Traveller in Eternity*, Regency Press, London and New York, 1956, reprinted in 1975

Harrison, Peter and Mary, *Life Before Birth*, Macdonald Futura & Co. London & Sydney, 1983

Hittleman, Richard, *Guide to Yoga Meditation*, Bantam Books, London, New York, Toronto, 1969

Hoyle, Fred and Wickramasinghe, N. C., *Diseases From Space*, Sphere Books, London, 1979

Iyengar, B. K. S., *Light on Yoga*, Allen & Unwin, London, 1968

Jaquin, Noel, *The Hand Speaks*, Sagar Publications, New Delhi, 1973

Meek, George W. and Harris, Bertha, *Seance To Science*, Regency Press, London and New York, 1973

Ouseley, S. G. J., *The Power of the Rays: The Science of Colour Healing*, L. N. Fowler & Co. Ltd., London 1975

Reiker, Hans-Ulrich, *The Yoga of Light*, The Dawn Horse Press, California, 1976

Schul, Bill, *The Psychic Power of Animals*, Coronet Books, London, 1977

Wolff, Charlotte, *The Hand In Psychological Diagnosis*, Sagar Publications, New Delhi, 1972

FINDING A MEDIUM

Appointments can be made with mediums at the following organizations:

The College of Psychic Studies, 16 Queensberry Place, London SW7 2EB. Tel. 071 589 3292

The Spiritualist Association of Great Britain, 33 Belgrave Square, London SW1X 8QB. Tel. 071 235 3351

FINDING A HEALER

Please write to:

National Federation of Spiritual Healers,
Old Manor Farm Studio,
Church Street,
Sunbury-on-Thames
TW16 6RG.
Tel. 0932 783164

If you or someone you know is in need of absent healing or would like to learn more about the tapes mentioned in this book, please write to me:

Betty Shine, PO Box 1009, Hassocks, West Sussex, BN6 8XS

I have been a vitamin and mineral therapist for 36 years and have willingly and freely given of my knowledge throughout those years. However, for various reasons, I have now decided to supply my own Betty Shine Health Products. These include vitamin and mineral supplements, scarves for colour healing and a pocket-size self-help diary. Further products will be introduced during 1992.

As well as the usual information, the 1992 self-help diary will include my photograph, requested by many people, the whole of the *Mind Magic* vitamin and mineral and remedy chapters and selected exercises so that you can carry them wherever you go.

For further information about Betty Shine Health Products, please write separately to:

Betty Shine Health Products, PO Box 1009, Hassocks, BN6 8XS

S.A.E. PLEASE!

MIND TO MIND

BY BETTY SHINE

Betty Shine is a remarkable woman. Her extraordinary gifts – a clairvoyant ability to diagnose medically, her healing powers and her discovery of 'mind energy' – have made her one of Britain's foremost healers.

Mind to Mind tells her story. Like Betty herself, it is cheerful, down-to-earth and full of humour. It reveals how she became aware of her gifts and how she has used her experiences of mind energy to help others. Illustrated with a wide variety of examples and case histories, this is a uniquely helpful and practical book by a woman whose powers have been a comfort and an inspiration to countless numbers of people.

'It is a positive, optimistic book, which I am sure will be a great encouragement to anyone who believes that the mind is capable of much more than we can presently dream of'
Michael Aspel

'This is a rare book, written by a rare person. I know that you will enjoy reading it'
Michael Bentine

'Full of fascinating case histories'
Guardian

'Fascinating and very readable . . . compelling and informative . . . written with humility and intelligence'
Psychic News

0 552 13378 7

A SELECTION OF OTHER FINE TITLES
AVAILABLE FROM CORGI BOOKS

THE PRICES SHOWN BELOW WERE CORRECT AT THE TIME OF GOING TO
PRESS. HOWEVER TRANSWORLD PUBLISHERS RESERVE THE RIGHT TO
SHOW NEW RETAIL PRICES ON COVERS WHICH MAY DIFFER FROM
THOSE PREVIOUSLY ADVERTISED IN THE TEXT OR ELSEWHERE.

☐	13492	9	OPEN YOUR MIND	*Michael Bentine* £3.99
☐	99160	0	FIRE FROM WITHIN	*Carlos Casteneda* £5.99
☐	99332	8	THE POWER OF SILENCE	*Carlos Casteneda* £5.99
☐	09828	0	THE PROPHECIES OF NOSTRADAMUS	*Erika Cheetham* £4.99
☐	12299	8	THE FURTHER PROPHECIES OF NOSTRADAMUS	*Erika Cheetham* £3.50
☐	11487	1	LIFE AFTER DEATH	*Neville Randall* £3.99
☐	13378	7	MIND TO MIND	*Betty Shine* £3.99
☐	13046	X	BEYOND THE OCCULT	*Colin Wilson* £5.99
☐	13429	5	THE AFTER DEATH EXPERIENCE	*Ian Wilson* £4.99

All Corgi/Bantam Books are available at your bookshop or newsagent, or can be
ordered from the following address:
Corgi/Bantam Books,
Cash Sales Department,
P.O. Box 11, Falmouth, Cornwall TR10 9EN

UK and B.F.P.O. customers please send a cheque or postal order (no currency) and
allow £1.00 for postage and packing for the first book plus 50p for the second book
and 30p for each additional book to a maximum charge of £3.00 (7 books plus).

Overseas customers, including Eire, please allow £2.00 for postage and packing for
the first book plus £1.00 for the second book and 50p for each subsequent title
ordered.

NAME (Block Letters) ....

ADDRESS ....

....